Making Good Money in Belfast

The story of ten social economy businesses

by Sammy Douglas, Maurice Kinkead
and Geoffrey Ready

Avec Publishing • Belfast

Avec Publishing
Avalon House
278 Newtownards Road
Belfast
BT4 1HE

First published 2006

Edited, designed and typeset by Avec Publishing.

ISBN 0-9553186-0-2
978-0-9553186-0-3

Foreword: Growing Sustainability

The demand for the sustainability of community and voluntary sector organisations has been around for well over a decade now, and more often than not is based on mutual deception between funders and those groups that receive grant funding.

On the one hand grant applicants reassure the funding bodies that undoubtedly they will be financially viable within the next three year period through their own income generating ventures; while the funders, for their part, rarely interrogate these assurances too closely. And so things continue on their merry way.

However, one of the areas of interest that has introduced a new escape route out of this cycle is the social economy. There is of course a danger that social economy just becomes a new buzzword, and that there is an over expectation about just how much it can deliver in terms of the self-sustainability of community and voluntary organisations.

Notwithstanding this there has been a tradition within the sector in Northern Ireland of being enterprising and innovative. One only has to look at the community-based cooperative development movement of the 1970s and 80s; the establishment of centres from Ebrington in the Waterside to Farset in Belfast; the diversity of rural enterprise ventures; and the contracting for the provision of services by community and voluntary groups. Whether the initiative is based on property service enterprise or simply a good idea the seeds of the social economy approach took ready root.

But what is the social economy? From the viewpoint of the Community Foundation for Northern Ireland it encompasses organisations that share certain characteristics:

- They will have social goals and will have emerged to fulfil a social need
- They will be governed by an inclusive ownership structure – directed by those people that the organisation is seeking to serve, or by a non profit-taking organisation representing the interests of that group
- They will have a significant enterprise orientation

Getting the balance right between the social motivation and the economic emphasis has often proved to be tricky – but as this book shows us, it is not impossible.

Clearly the decision to become a social economy organisation – or to develop an orientation in this direction should not be taken lightly. And yet the increasing awareness of the very real long-term challenge of sustainability is encouraging an ever increasing number of organisations to explore this option. This publication will help them. As such it is to be welcomed.

Avila Kilmurray
Director
Community Foundation for Northern Ireland

Acknowledgements

The creation of this book, and the associated website, was only possible with the financial support of the Community Foundation for Northern Ireland, distributing resources from the Local Community Fund.

The Community Foundation for Northern Ireland has been an active supporter of the social economy for many years and its support for this project is much appreciated.

We would also acknowledge the active participation of the social economy projects featured in this publication and thank them for making time and personnel available for interviews, photographs and so forth, especially within such a tight timescale.

We have attempted to ensure the accuracy of all the accounts of the various projects, but where this is not the case, we will make corrections within the online version.

Thanks are also due to Kerry Moreland for help in compiling much of the information in the appendices and for ongoing administrative support.

Finally, thanks to all the many people and organisations, only some of whom are referred to in this publication, from whom we have learned much about the social economy.

We should also add that the views and interpretations reflected within this publication are those of the authors and do not necessarily reflect the views of organisations mentioned within the book, of Community Foundation of Northern Ireland, nor of Avec Publishing and associated companies.

Photography

Most of the photographs contained within this publication have be taken by Nigel Hunter (www.nigelhunter.com), although a number have also been provided by participating social economy projects.

Contents

Introduction

This book focuses on ten social economy projects with which we are familiar, all operating in disadvantaged areas of Belfast and all of which are, or hope soon to be, 'making good money'.

They are certainly not the only social economy projects operating across the city, and have not been chosen because they are the best, but because we believe that they have much to teach us about running a social enterprise. They have been chosen because they appear to be working effectively and may inspire or provide practical ideas and help to others who are thinking of starting similar activities.

The social economy is diverse and much has already been said and written about how to define it. That is not a debate we intend to enter here but suffice it to say that the projects in this book, apart from operating in disadvantaged areas of Belfast, have at least two things in common: (1) they operate on a non-profit taking model; that is, any profit made does not find its way into the pocket of any private individuals, but is used for some community benefit; and (2) they are all providing a product or service on a commercial basis.

Some are indeed standalone businesses operating freely in the marketplace and 'making good money' for their 'owners', which are usually charities addressing social needs within the city.

Others, such as the Orchardville Business Centre, are achieving their social aims through the business activity itself, and while they may not be 'profitable' in the full sense, they are making a very significant and 'good' contribution to their own sustainability.

The book is structured into three sections. The first and main section includes the stories of the ten social economy companies, presented in a manner to be practically helpful and informative.

We hope each article will provide enough information to give you some idea of whether you want to find out more, and we have enclosed some detailed contact information to allow you to follow this up in whatever way you think appropriate. All the projects covered in this book have comprehensive websites and all can accommodate 'good practice visits', usually at a modest cost.

The second section of the book addresses some issues and themes which the authors have come across in managing their own social economy business and in talking to other social entrepreneurs as they have researched this book.

These articles are by no means intended to be the last word on the various topics but are primarily based on personal experience and as such may add something to the ongoing debate about managing social economy activities.

The third and last section tries to provide some practical information in terms of organisations, further reading and websites that we have come across in trying to find information for our own use and in preparing this book.

It is perhaps also worth saying, though hopefully not by way of excuse for any poor quality workmanship, that this book has been researched, written and printed within a period of about six weeks. The main reason for this was the restricted time available within which the funding could be used to cover the cost of printing.

Associated with this book is a website which you will find at www.makinggoodmoney.org. On the website you will find a downloadable PDF version of this entire book as well as PDFs of the individual chapters.

We will also shortly be adding other stories of similar projects in Belfast and beyond that we were not able to include in the printed book.

You will also find direct links to the websites of all the social enterprises mentioned in this book and others that we have since come across.

Making Good Money in Belfast... on the web

www.makinggoodmoney.org

Buy the book online
Download entire book (PDF)
Download individual chapters (PDFs)
Read more stories of successful social economy projects

It was a strange phone call. "If you call this number in the states," my friend said, "they will send you $5000 to work up a business plan for a telecottage in east Belfast." I said OK and hung up. I didn't even know what a telecottage was, but I was sure east Belfast could do with one!

This was how Sammy Douglas, former chairman of the East Belfast Partnership, remembers the start of Avec Solutions, or as it was then known, ECOM Management.

A group in west Belfast, with support from a donor in the US, had put together a proposal to Belfast City Council to fund a telecottage project, but such were the politics in Belfast in the mid-1990s that funding was unlikely to be granted unless there was a 'matching' grant for a project in the 'other community'. As a result of this process, a grant of almost £60,000 was duly received to establish an east Belfast telecottage which would provide IT information and support to local businesses and groups.

Avec Solutions

ICT consultancy and support services

It may be hard to believe now, but in the mid-1990s in Belfast email and the internet were rarely found in your average office and the initial idea was for the telecottage to provide an email service with local businesses and groups then calling in to collect a printout of their message – the hope was it would impress others!

Thankfully, those involved in East Belfast Partnership who were tasked with setting up the telecottage could see that rapid change was on the way and decided, in conjunction with the council, that the best way to provide IT support to local groups and businesses, as well as making the activity sustainable in the long term, was to establish the project as an ICT consultancy, and so ECOM Management was born.

The new initiative was launched by Sir Reg Empey, chair of the city council development committee (and a future minister for the economy) in February 1999, although for various reasons at the time of launch the business had no staff. Richard Rea, a self-employed IT consultant who had helped us set up the business, had by this stage moved on.

However, soon afterwards the current managing consultant, Geoffrey Ready, was appointed as ECOM's first full time IT consultant. There were of course no clients but Geoffrey's first task was to set up the new Microsoft server based network for the parent company, the East Belfast Partnership, leading to our first invoice (even the parent company can't have work done for nothing!).

Facts & Figures

Avec Solutions
Company limited by guarantee
Avalon House
278 Newtownards Road
Belfast BT4 1HE
T: 028 9045 9000
www.avecsolutions.com
www.avecsolutions.net
Contact person: Geoffrey Ready
E: geoffrey@avecsolutions.com

Financial information
Turnover (05/06) £283,000
Profit (05/06) £15,000
Employees: 6 f/t

Services
ICT consultancy
Social economy management consultancy
Finance and accountancy services
Hardware and software sales
Network design and installation
Contract support packages
Web development
Open source enterprise applications
VoIP phone systems

Internet services
ADSL broadband internet access
Domain name registration
Web and email hosting

Managing consultant Geoffrey Ready meets with a client

there was little money available for marketing, but the client list began to grow through word-of-mouth recommendations

An IT suite had been set up, with various hardware and software installed, and this was then opened on a 'drop in' basis to show those interested what was possible. Alongside this facility Geoffrey also began a series of free seminars on various ICT related topics, which proved very popular.

However, the company was aware that a grant of £60,000 would not last long, as about half of this was used for setup costs, and it set itself the task of breaking even by the end of the first year.

The drop-in facility and free seminar series had raised awareness of what was available through ECOM and soon customers were approaching Geoffrey looking for consultancy and support. There was little money available for marketing, but the client list began to grow through word-of-mouth recommendations and as the end of the first year approached there were more customers than the business could handle. The client list had been further boosted during 2000 as the local community sector had acquired a significant grant allowing it to directly purchase ICT support from ECOM for local community groups.

At this stage LEDU, the small business support agency, was approached and a small grant was made available to take on an additional employee. The business was now growing, both through direct sales of ICT support services to a growing client list, and also by competing for some grant-funded support projects to third parties.

After a couple of successful years, during which the business built up an operating reserve of about £70,000 and contributed around £100,000 of profit to its parent company, a decision was then taken in 2001 which was to have a dramatic effect on the future of the company.

The decision was to seek to grow the company, particularly in the 'primary market' of medium sized non-profit organisations, but also to develop the market in the private sector, focusing on businesses providing professional services. This happened alongside a decision to become less dependent on delivering large grant-funded projects.

To ensure that the company had sufficient resources to meet the expected demand, two additional posts were created, giving a team of a managing consultant, two IT consultants and two IT assistants. This move to grow the business coincided with the decision to change the name of the business to Avec Solutions, to avoid confusion with another IT company with a similar name to ECOM.

While the decision to grow the client list was certainly successful in terms of attracting many new customers, it also came within 'a hair's breadth' of sinking the business. The company had budgeted for a loss in order to make a significant investment in growth during the 2002-03 year, but as the end of the third quarter approached, losses had reached £60,000, using up virtually all the reserves built up in previous years. Although the business had donated £100,000 of profit to its charitable parent company, these funds were no longer available to the business, which was in serious danger of folding if urgent action was not taken.

And indeed urgent, and difficult, action was taken. Two staff were made redundant, existing staff relocated to much smaller and cheaper offices, other savings were made and the business 'pulled out all the stops' to gain new business. It also became 'harder' in terms of not taking on less profitable work and more vigorously chasing bad debt, especially from some non-profit organisations who were perhaps abusing the company's goodwill.

'we learned more about running a business through responding successfully to our mistakes than we ever could through any number of management courses'

During the final quarter no further losses were incurred and by 2003-04 the business moved back into profitability, with a leaner operation and much healthier client list. It had had a serious 'scare', but had emerged all the stronger.

As managing consultant Geoffrey can now add with hindsight: "We know we were taking a risk in growing the business, and perhaps with inexperience we underestimated the cost. However, we learned more about running a business through responding successfully to our mistakes than we ever could through any number of management courses."

Future plans

Having now established itself as a leading provider of ICT services within the Northern Ireland voluntary sector, and with a significant and growing private sector client list, Avec Solutions has no intention of 'resting on its laurels'.

Adding to its network installation, contract support, web design and hosting services, Avec has recognised the growing integration of data and voice technology and has now developed the necessary expertise and experience to implement fully integrated telephone systems for clients using Voice over Internet Protocol (VoIP) technology. It has also recently launched its own ADSL broadband service.

Avec is also aware that, in addition to providing high quality ICT support to its clients, the business has a responsibility to achieve a profitable return for its 'owner' East Belfast Partnership and is determined to do so by continuing to grow the client list.

However, it also recognises the importance of maintaining and indeed improving the quality of service provided and to that end it has recently appointed a customer care co-ordinator and made customer care the direct responsibility of a specific senior manager.

In addition, with the relative success of Avec Solutions and associated companies, there has been considerable demand from others in the social economy sector to provide practical help, advice and support. As a result, Avec Solutions is now offering such support on a consultancy basis, although being careful not to take away from its core business of ICT support.

Avec's network engineers provide contract support to more than 50 clients

Lessons learned

According to Geoffrey Ready, many lessons have been learned over the past seven years, with perhaps the most valuable being learned 'the hard way'. These would include:

Don't forget the basics: the business has definitely learned through hard experience that keeping a clear focus on profit and in doing so watching costs, credit control and cashflow, is of paramount importance. The simple fact is that, if the company does not make a profit, it will go out of business and be of no value to either its owner or customers.

Customer is king: in a service business such as Avec's, the company has learned to focus on customer needs and indeed has now based its marketing around quality and customer service with the vast majority of new clients coming through recommendation from existing customers.

Customer care doesn't mean being 'soft': while Avec understands the grant related issues faced by many non-profit clients, and seeks to work supportively with them when for example grant payments may be late, it has also learned to distinguish between this and being taken advantage of. Indeed, in a few situations it has not been afraid to threaten legal action to secure payment for services provided, although this is still seen as a last resort.

Grants are no substitute for clients: Avec has delivered a number of projects over the years based on grant funding, but has learned not to be dependent on them. Indeed at times the bureaucracy surrounding the grant has made it difficult to focus on the core business and Avec is now hesitant to take on work where grants are directly involved. Avec sees its future as built on providing an excellent quality of service to a growing and loyal customer base, although it will certainly be open to delivering externally funded projects where it sees a definite opportunity.

Computer Connections

Located in Belfast City centre, Computer Connections offers a wide range of IT support services. A social economy enterprise, established by the Ashton Centre in north Belfast, the company has extensive community and commercial experience of delivering hardware, software and networking support. It currently provides support contracts to a wide range of organisations throughout Northern Ireland, offering the following services:

Hardware and software installation
Customised IT solutions
Service contracts and support
Network and server installation
Web design
Web and email hosting
Drop-in repair centre
Computer Connections shop

Contact details
Contact person: Robin Montgomery
Computer Connections
191 Donegall Street
Belfast BT1 2FJ
T: 028 9032 4633
F: 028 9032 4644
E: info@computer-connections.info
W: www.computer-connections.info

If you are looking for smart, good value accommodation in Belfast, Springfield Road might not immediately spring to mind. However, with the opening of Farset International, an impressive, community owned and managed facility, that is exactly what you find.

Set in private grounds on a small wildfowl reserve, Farset International boasts a panoramic view of the city by day, with the amazing lights of city life by night. The project is a spin-off from its parent company, Farset Youth and Community Development Ltd, which was established in 1982 to provide job opportunities and training for young people.

Jackie Hewitt was a key driver behind the creation of Farset International

Farset International

First class good value accommodation

The idea for the hostel was first mooted in the 1980s during youth exchange visits between young people from West Belfast and their peers from a number of European cities.

At the time, mainly as a result of political unrest, youth hostel accommodation in Belfast left much to be desired. Apart from only finding basic backpack facilities at many of the venues, restrictions meant that alcohol was generally forbidden on the premises and lights had to be out for 9.30pm – not much fun for young men and women from other European cities where they had become used to modern facilities and being treated like adults!

Contrasted sharply with the superb accommodation on offer to the young people from Belfast on their European exchange visits, the hostel facilities in Belfast embarrassed local community leaders.

As Belfast began to return to peace and normality in the 1990s, the hostel idea was resurrected and driven by Jackie Hewitt, a well known community leader from the Shankill area of Belfast. He was supported throughout the process by the Reverend Roy Magee, the chairman of Farset YCD and also a key figure in the Northern Ireland peace process, along with board member Barney McCaughey.

They identified the potential upturn in the depressed Northern Ireland tourism industry and the need for quality conferencing, banqueting and overnight accommodation at affordable prices.

It was also recognised that after many years of the troubles, West Belfast's reputation had created a curiosity factor for large numbers of potential visitors to the city who would be interested in organised cultural tours to see the famous Belfast murals and learn about local political ideologies and conflict.

After identifying a derelict site on the picturesque banks of the Springfield dam overlooking Belfast, Jackie and his fellow directors of Farset YCD began to explore the feasibility of building a hostel using local labour.

Difficulties

The initial plan was to build the facility through the Action for Community Enterprise (ACE) scheme, a government sponsored work training programme that had been used by the organisation for a number of years.

Facts & Figures

Farset International Hostel
466 Springfield Road
Belfast BT12 7DW
T: 028 9089 9833
F: 028 9089 9839
E: info@farsetinternational.co.uk
W: www.farsetinternational.co.uk
Contact person: Jackie Hewitt

Accommodation
38 ensuite bedrooms
3 fully equipped conference rooms
The Foundry restaurant for evening meals (on request)
24-hour Secure Parking.

Financial information
Turnover (2005) £400,000
Employees: 27

Farset has become a successful conference centre

However, as with so many social economy projects, it wasn't all plain sailing, and the first setback resulted in the collapse of the ACE scheme as a result of a change in government policy before any construction had commenced.

Farset International, which is more of a budget hotel than a hostel, has been a major success defying the critics and cynics as its reputation as a quality location continues to grow

Added to this, potential funders including the Northern Ireland Tourist Board and government departments were not convinced of the need or the potential success of a hostel facility located in the upper Springfield Road, an interface area of Belfast that had borne the brunt of over 25 years of political upheaval and community conflict.

Undeterred, the organisers pushed forward with their plans for the innovative scheme to bring jobs and revitalisation to an area that had become synonymous with violence and division. This self-assurance had been forged from their experience of developing and managing social and economic regeneration projects during the worst period of civil unrest throughout the 1980s. They had successfully developed an enterprise centre for small business incubation units in the vicinity as well as a number of mediation and reconciliation programmes which had helped to bring a sense of normality to the area.

The hostel project received a real boost and encouragement when the International Fund for Ireland (IFI) agreed to commit substantial financial help to the venture, subject to approval and support by government in the form of an economic appraisal. Key to this support was Hugh McCloskey, the IFI development consultant who became a champion of the project and influenced other funders who were wavering in their commitment. Born and bred in west Belfast, he was convinced of the need for such a facility and his commitment and dedication was to become a crucial factor in the eventual success of the project.

But the whole application process dragged on for many months with a huge amount of work put in by Farset directors, most of it on a voluntary basis. Eventually, it became clear that the group's endeavours were being frustrated as they found themselves pushed from pillar to post and burdened with the sheer weight of bureaucracy and in particular the appraisal process.

Indeed the organisers felt that some officials in government were actually opposed to their exciting plans for a flagship social economy project, as they were being forced through so many hoops. Also, as a result of these many delays, the original costs of the project continued to increase as the appraisal process went on.

To add insult to injury, the local further and higher education institution pulled the plug on their commitment to the project at the last minute. They had indicated an interest in becoming an integral part of the initiative, training unemployed people for the growing catering industry. They would also have been a major tenant in the new building providing much needed income for the venture.

These negative developments left board members reeling from the shock and gave ammunition to the cynics who appeared to be looking for an excuse to maintain and justify their position of opposition.

Eventually, the patience of Farset directors ran out and a letter was sent to all the major funders and supporters informing them that the plans for the development had been shelved.

This caused shockwaves within the public and political sectors and it was at this juncture that political intervention by two politicians added a new energy and optimism into the seemingly hopeless situation that Farset faced.

Councillor Fred Cobain and Sir Reg Empey, who had become the Minister for Enterprise, Trade and Investment in the New Northern Ireland Executive in 1999, met with the disillusioned Farset board and encouraged them not to give up but to persevere and pursue their dreams. A meeting was convened at the Assembly buildings in Stormont, attended by various government officials, and a deal was hammered out that gave the green light to fund the project.

Success

After many years of frustration Farset International finally opened its doors for business in 2003. The project costs of £2.25 million were met by a cocktail of funding from IFI, the Department of Social Department, Belfast European Partnership Board, as well as a loan from Ulster Community Investment Trust.

To date Farset International, which is more of a budget hotel than a hostel, has been a major success defying the critics and cynics as its reputation as a quality location continues to grow. The average occupancy rate since the official opening has exceeded 60% which is remarkable achievement considering the venture has been established in untried territory.

With a healthy turnover of nearly £400,000 in 2005, the Farset Company is also one of the biggest employers in the area with a staff team of 27 – a remarkable feat in one of the worst unemployment black spots in Belfast.

Patrons come from across the island of Ireland and international visitors have been flocking to the venue which offers ensuite twin rooms with TVs and tea and coffee making facilities. There is also a residents' lounge, a self-catering kitchen, laundry and secure parking. The Foundry Restaurant and Mackie's Bistro serve up excellent food and can cater for large and small on-site conferences.

US Senator George Mitchell, who had played an important role in the Northern Ireland peace process, paid tribute to the excellent facility and the role it continues to play in cross-community and cross-border events

At one such conference in 2005, US Senator George Mitchell, who had played such an important role in the Northern Ireland peace process, paid tribute to the excellent facility and the role it continues to play in cross-community and cross-border events.

In addition, the hosting of local and international peace-building programmes has been an important aspect in the growth of the facility as a neutral and safe venue.

Future Plans

As a result of the peace process, Belfast has undoubtedly become a vibrant and modern cosmopolitan European city, re-inventing itself as it emerges and develops from its unique past. Interestingly, the word Belfast is the anglicisation of Beal Feirste which if translated directly into English would read "mouth of the Farset", the Farset being one of the smaller rivers that flow through Belfast from the adjacent Antrim mountains into the River Lagan.

The members of Farset International recognise the huge potential of increasing visitor numbers to Belfast,, particularly in the cultural tourism which it has to offer, and are keen to exploit the warm hospitality and

Farset manager Ruth Quigley meets with Jackie Hewitt

friendliness for which its people are famous. In this regard, the location of the hostel provides a safe and welcoming neutral venue, with a growing reputation as a popular accommodation destination.

A number of community organisations in the vicinity have developed plans in association with Farset to revitalise the adjoining Springfield dam as a tourist attraction by stocking it with trout.

As well as developing tourism, Farset aims to build on experiences and skills gained during the troubles in international mediation and conflict resolution, particularly with growing international interest in how the Northern Ireland peace process has evolved.

Lessons learned

Jackie Hewitt, who is now in overall control of Farset, highlighted some of the lessons that he and fellow board members learned as a result of their experiences.

He pointed to the vital role that project champions played at key stages over the years and expressed his gratitude to those "friendly faces" in organisations that were a constant help and encouragement during the difficult days.

He acknowledged that the project would never have got off the ground without the political support mentioned earlier. He is also keen to mention that this support extended across the religious and political divide from people like Alex Maskey, the former Sinn Fein Lord Mayor of Belfast.

And while there were many months of frustration and at times, despair with government officials, he has nonetheless appreciated the problems and dilemmas that confront funders and government departments, particularly when dealing with a new idea in an untried location such as west Belfast that has had a history of political and community upheaval.

However, while during the entire process the message from the highest echelons of government was about "taking risks for peace", Hewitt noted that the Farset experience clearly showed that "there is a civil service mentality that militates against officials taking risks lest they find themselves facing a Public Accounts Committee".

This attitude of vacillation and indecision was at the heart of the frustrations and difficulties experienced over the years resulting in the costs of the project spiralling, a situation which created a continuous, vicious circle of fluctuation and uncertainty.

On the other hand, there were people who were willing to take calculated risks in organisations such as the International Fund for Ireland and the Belfast European Partnership Board, funders that believed in the scheme and were willing to give Farset 'a fair wind' by offering vital support at key milestones during the process. And it was this encouragement that helped the Farset board members and staff to hold their nerve and cling to their vision during the bleakest of times.

One of the people who epitomised this spirit of doggedness and determination was the late Ann Brown MBE. Ann was the Farset administrator, a constant tower of strength who put her heart and soul into the development of the project but sadly, she never lived to see the completion of the impressive building.

As Jackie Hewitt admitted, "without Ann's input, the whole scheme may never have got off the ground". As a testimony to her contribution to Farset, the Ann Brown Suite was named after her and there are plans for a trust to be established in her name to celebrate her life.

Farset Youth and Community Development

Farset Youth and Community Development Ltd was established in 1982 in response to the need identified by local community workers to provide young people with a community facility for work and training. This facility was set up as part of the government's Youth Training Programme.

Following the reorganisation of youth training provision, Farset became involved in the development of the Action for Community Employment (ACE) programme and became the largest ACE provider in Northern Ireland employing over 150 people.

Since 1985 Farset has been based on the Springfield Road on Belfast's peace line providing a focus for employment, training, reconciliation, community development and economic regeneration within the surrounding communities.

Farset's management committee has been very active and brings together a multitude of skills and talents. Tens of thousands of pounds are saved annually by their voluntary input.

Farset strives to respond in a meaningful way to the needs of the community. Its primary aim is to tackle the problems of chronic unemployment and social deprivation that afflict the communities of north and west Belfast.

Long term unemployment has been extremely high in these areas for many years with many families suffering from the effects of third generation unemployment.

Farset provides a variety of projects designed to address the social, economic and physical needs of the community. Special emphasis is placed on the needs of the most vulnerable such as the elderly, the disabled, children and young people at risk.

In the midst of one of the most socially and economically disadvantaged areas of Belfast you will find Kinder Kids Day Care, one of the first community-owned and managed full daycare projects in the city.

Situated in the New Lodge area, it provides a high quality childcare provision for 60 children aged between six months and 12 years per day. Fully registered with social services, this is a much needed service in an area characterised by high levels of socio-economic deprivation with a high proportion of lone parents. Statistics show that the New Lodge area has a higher than average proportion of children and young people, and a higher level of unemployed households with dependent children, than most other areas of Belfast.

Kinder Kids

Community-owned daycare facility

To facilitate parents, the centre is open between 8am and 6pm each weekday, providing both part time and full time quality care and development to suit individual circumstances. To deliver such a significant service, the centre currently has a workforce of 21 including a manager, an administrator and 19 qualified staff.

Early days

This impressive initiative is the brainchild of Ashton Community Trust (ACT), a registered charity formed in 1992 under a trust deed before being established as a company limited by guarantee in 1998.

According to Paul Roberts, who has been with the trust as overall manager of the Ashton Centre since 1994 and the driving force behind Kinder Kids Day Care, the need for a quality daycare centre was a natural progression from the trust's role in the local community.

"It kicked off because, from the very start when the Ashton Centre was set up, we were providing jobs, but local people weren't able to access them because they didn't have the skills.

"We therefore set about providing training and realised there were problems about accessibility. Accessible and affordable childcare became a major issue so initially we provided a small crèche in one room. That's where it developed."

From those early days of providing much needed crèche facilities, an afterschools club was established in 1998, operating as a separate project. It was at this stage that the organisation began to explore the potential for an amalgamation of the various childcare support projects into a more effective and sustainable operation.

Reacting to funding opportunities, research in the form of a feasibility study was carried out to identify the potential of Ashton providing a full daycare facility. The study indicated the need not only for additional and significant space but the potential for a large financial commitment to the project from Ashton's financial reserves.

Facts & Figures

Kinder Kids Day Care
5 Churchill Street
Belfast
BT15 2BP
T: 028 9074 2255 (ext 222)
F: 028 9074 2255
E: info@ashtoncentre.com
W: www.ashtoncentre.com

Contacts
Paul Roberts
Christine McKeown (childcare manager)

Financial information
Turnover (2005): £320,000
Childcare places: 60 per day
Employees: 21

Ashton director Paul Roberts meets with childcare manager Christine McKeown

In 2000 Kinder Kids Day Care was set up and, using reserves which had been built up over the years through various income generation schemes, Ashton decided to employ a childcare manager to take the project forward.

As many social economy projects have discovered, the decision to employ a full time professional manager was to prove crucial in the overall development of the project.

The manager was able to focus entirely on managing and developing the fledgling Kinder Kids Day Care initiative, establishing a close and important working relationship with the local social services department and effectively targeting the project for local people, primarily women, from inner north Belfast.

As a result of its community base, the service also provides a link with other local training and employment providers. In this way it acts as a signpost for local people to access training and employment opportunities, while at the same time providing local, accessible and affordable childcare provision 'on the doorstep'.

Future plans

The initiative has been such an overwhelming success, obviously meeting a clear need, that Kinder Kids doesn't need to advertise for children to take up available places. Indeed, there is currently a waiting list that could double the present number of children if the facility had the space.

As a result of the experience gained from running Kinder Kids Day Care, there are plans to open up a similar centre on the Cliftonville Road, in an adjacent area of north Belfast.

The new initiative will be run as a viable social enterprise offering quality childcare for up to 70 children.

fully registered with social services, this is a much needed service in an area characterised by high levels of socio-economic deprivation with a high proportion of lone parents

Lessons learned

According to Paul Roberts, the appointment of a full time day care manager was probably the most important strategic decision they made in addressing the growing demand for childcare provision: "The manager brought commitment, passion, skills and a professionalism to the overall scheme of things. To be honest, the project would probably have not happened without her."

This appointment ensured the running of the project in a professional and efficient manner. It also meant going the extra mile to guarantee a safe and quality service in an industry where guidelines regarding staff to children ratios are often exceeded.

The Ashton board of directors were conscious of the need to run the daycare facility as a financially viable social enterprise. "We needed to do it in such a fashion that it wouldn't always be a matter of relying on grant funding or a drain on our hard earned financial reserves," revealed Paul Roberts.

Another important factor in Kinder Kids' development was the introduction of the working family tax credit, which for the first time made full daycare affordable in areas such as New Lodge.

It also enabled the project to 'wash its own face' and in 2005 it made a slight profit from a turnover of around £320,000.

Yet unlike some private sector daycare facilities, the working conditions for staff are very impressive: the facility employs a fully unionised workforce and pays better wages and pensions than similar private schemes. This is certainly not daycare 'on the cheap' just because it is in a disadvantaged community.

The involvement of the local community has been another critical factor in the success of the venture to date. The Ashton vision of "a safe, prosperous and caring community where residents have pride and a sense of ownership" is central to the running of the daycare centre.

The marketing approach of the centre is based upon the community ethos of the trust, which has an established profile within the area.

unlike some private sector daycare facilities, the working conditions for staff are very impressive: the facility employs a fully unionised workforce and pays better wages and pensions than similar private schemes

This has meant that word of mouth has been the most effective means of advertising the service and ensuring that places are filled with support from local residents thereby ensuring future sustainability.

This is certainly the case with the afterschools provision, an essential element of a comprehensive daycare service as it removes barriers for local people who may wish to access training or employment or become involved in community development activities.

Childcare is thus seen as central to the work of the trust and key to the social and economic regeneration of the area.

A visit to the daycare centre where dozens of local kids learn and play in a safe and healthy environment would certainly convince visitors that the trust is living out its mission "to promote positive change and improve the quality of life of the north Belfast community".

Ashton Centre

Ashton Community Trust (ACT) is a registered charity and was formed in 1992 under a trust deed, before being established as a company limited by guarantee in 1998.

Over its 15 year history, through the Ashton Centre, the trust has reacted to the needs of the local community and the emphasis of the work has shifted accordingly. The initial phase as a community co-operative gave way to a greater concentration on economic, social and business development.

In the past 10 years the balance has shifted towards the role of a development agency, proactive in a range of areas affecting the local community, such as employment, health, education and social needs.

At all times the Ashton Centre has maintained a strong community development ethos, with an emphasis on responding to and serving the needs of the local population

The centre, based in the Churchill Street area of New Lodge, where Kinder Kids Day Care is also located, was conceived as a community initiative in 1985 and was originally based in a small office on the nearby Antrim Road.

The current centre opened for business in 1991 as a Centre for Enterprise and Community Development, serving the New Lodge area of north Belfast. These new premises had been built through grant funding and loans from the International Fund for Ireland and Community Economic Regeneration Scheme, as well as the proceeds of a share issue to local residents.

The centre comprises offices and meeting rooms for community use, with a number of ground floor shop units and workspace units.

It is owned by Ashton Centre Development Limited (ACDL), an industrial provident organisation, whose primary activity is the letting of office and workshop space to local businesses (both privately owned and social economy businesses) and community projects. Current tenants include a GP surgery, hairdressers, grocery shop and a car repair workshop.

Ashton Community Trust is also engaged in the delivery of various projects aimed at social and economic regeneration of the local area. These include employment outreach, education and training, social economy businesses, community empowerment, and childcare, all of which are further outlined on their comprehensive website.

The valuable work of the trust was publicly recognised in November 2005, when members travelled to London where they were awarded a commendation in the prestigious British Urban Regeneration Association Awards.

www.ashtoncentre.com

Paul Roberts and the Ashton Centre for enterprise and community development

Sometimes being in the right place at the right time is all it takes to get a business off the ground – well, maybe add to that a lot of perseverance and hard work. This was certainly the case with Landmark East.

Established by the East Belfast Partnership, an inter-sectoral regeneration agency, the original idea was that Landmark East would access public funds to develop derelict property in disadvantaged areas where the private sector had lost interest.

At the same time an asset base would be built which the Partnership could use to fund future urban regeneration.

Bloomfield House

Landmark East

Building for the future in East Belfast

While it was considering how to take the idea forward, the Partnership became aware of a property development project already partly developed by another organisation which had funding agreed in principle, but which for various reasons was not able to proceed. Enter the newly formed Landmark East with an offer to take the project on and the fledgling new business was on its way!

The concept behind Landmark East was to identify derelict sites and seek grant aid funding to develop them and bring them back into economic use within the community. The rationale for this was that if such properties could be developed they may act as a catalyst for the private sector also to invest in these areas.

As Landmark East was a not for profit company then the high level of grant aid was not an issue as such public funds would not find their way into private hands. Indeed, as Landmark East was owned by a charity committed to urban regeneration, any profit derived from such a project could end up being used for further regeneration.

While the concept appeared sound, its implementation was not as straightforward as property needed to be identified, acquired and then appropriate funding sourced. However, the decision was made to proceed and a number of people were identified to put the idea into action.

These included Sammy Douglas and Maurice Kinkead, the Chair and Chief Executive of East Belfast Partnership, Peter Osborne, the chair of the partnership's working group on the environment, Maggie Andrews, then director of East Belfast Community Development Agency, Colin Johnston, a property developer and finance director at the Bairds pharmacy group, Peter Lavery, a property developer (and major lottery winner), Ronnie Rutherford, a local businessman, and Gordon Wright, a local bank manager. Observers included Noel Scott and Michael Meenan from Making Belfast Work and Robin Hawe from the NI Housing Executive. The company was formed in June 1998 under the name of Landmark East.

Although the first project had more or less 'fallen into their lap' it took approximately two years and a multitude of meetings to get the funding

Facts & Figures

Landmark East
Company limited by guarantee
Avalon House, 278 Newtownards Road
Belfast BT4 1HE
T: 028 9045 9000
www.landmarkeast.com
Contact person: Maurice Kinkead
E: maurice@landmarkeast.com

Financial information
Asset value: £2 million
Borrowing: £400,000
Rental income: £120,000
Profit (04/05) £40,000
Employees: 1 f/t, 2 p/t

Property
Lagan Village Tower – 6000 sq ft
Bloomfield House – 8000 sq ft
Avalon House – 5000 sq ft

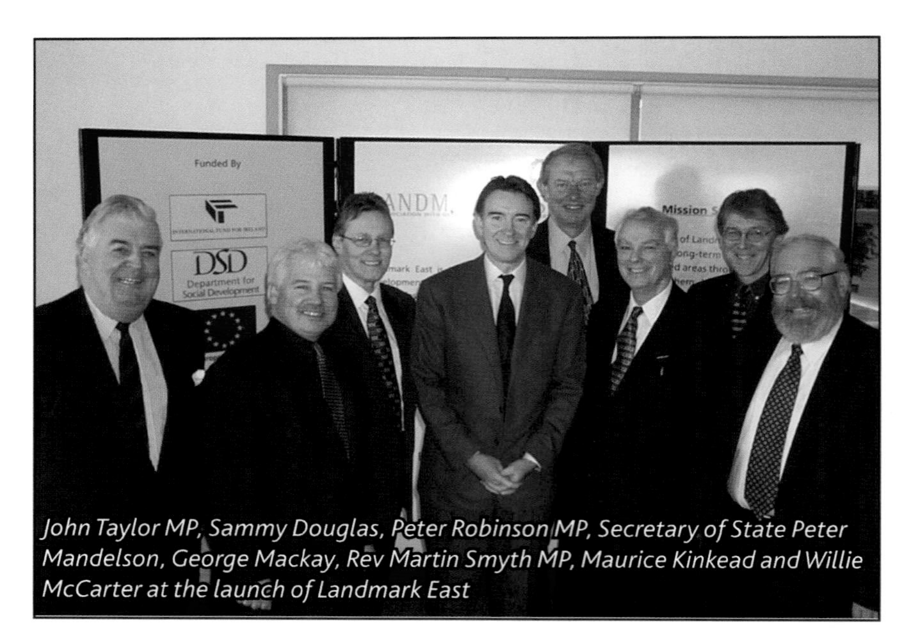

John Taylor MP, Sammy Douglas, Peter Robinson MP, Secretary of State Peter Mandelson, George Mackay, Rev Martin Smyth MP, Maurice Kinkead and Willie McCarter at the launch of Landmark East

package through economic appraisal. In late 2000 funding was released and Landmark East began building its first property, later named Lagan Village Tower. The total development cost was approximately £800,000, all of which was sourced through the International Fund for Ireland and the Department of the Environment (using EU funds). The building was completed on time and within budget in November 2001 and tenants were signed up for the entire space prior to completion.

as Landmark East was owned by a charity committed to urban regeneration, any profit derived from such a project could end up being used for further regeneration

Buoyed up by the success of the new project, other derelict properties were identified for the same treatment. These included a disused office building on the Newtownards Road, perhaps the most rundown main road in the city. This building had at one stage been the HQ for the Ulster Defence Association prior to it being declared an illegal organisation. The building, by now in a dangerous condition, was purchased and demolished and funding was sought to build a replacement building.

Today, with funding from the International Fund for Ireland and the Belfast Local Strategy Partnership (distributing EU funds), a brand new high specification social economy centre named Avalon House stands on this site.

Another building identified was a former well known shoe shop in what had once been the thriving commercial heart of East Belfast – Holywood Arches – but which was now seeing many of its businesses closing down or moving elsewhere. As this was a landmark building in East Belfast terms, the decision was taken to retain the existing structure and undertake a major refurbishment. Also, rather than seek 100% grant aid this time, the board of Landmark East took the same approach as any private developer, borrowing money from the bank and seeking an Urban Development Grant from government to fund the shortfall. The International Fund for Ireland continued to be very supportive and on this occasion was able to fund some of the fit-out costs for tenants and also purchase an adjacent property. On completion, the redeveloped Bloomfield House offered accommodation of approximately 8000 sq ft and was valued at £500,000, against which Landmark East had a loan of £350,000 and rental income of just over £50,000 a year.

With these developments complete Landmark East now has three properties totalling around 20,000 sq ft, all of which are fully occupied at the time of writing. And they are already working on their biggest project to date – a 25,000 sq ft multi-purpose centre in the Ballybeen housing estate, due for completion in mid 2008 at a cost in excess of £2 million.

Difficulties

Apart from the normal difficulties that any property developer would have, such as obtaining planning permission, dealing with cost overruns and disputes with contractors, Landmark East has also faced a number of challenges as a social economy company.

The Landmark East board recognise that without funding Landmark East would simply not exist – two of their three properties developed to date have benefited from virtually 100% public funding, which has given them an asset base on which to plan further development.

However, public funding quite rightly comes with many conditions, and at times complying with these, and the bureaucracy surrounding them, has been a major challenge. One economic appraisal took over two years to complete which meant a two year gap between agreeing to purchase the building and actually completing the sale!

Landmark East has also run into problems with funders mid-contract when the funder has considered that its compliance was not sufficient and release of funding was halted although the commitment to keep paying the contractor continued. At such times a very positive relationship with its bank, First Trust, has proved critically important.

The other main challenge Landmark East has faced has been in relation to decision-making. Buying and selling property, appointing professionals and contractors, managing each development – at times the structure of full time management staff and voluntary directors has struggled to cope with making effective decisions quickly, especially if funders also had to be consulted. Sometimes by the time the decision was made, the opportunity had long gone. It did however force the company's hand in looking for more effective decision-making processes.

with these developments complete Landmark East now has three properties totalling around 20,000 sq ft, all of which are fully occupied

Future plans

To date Landmark East has taken a somewhat conservative approach to development which has probably been right given the funding environment in which it was operating. It also means that at this stage it is in the happy position of having very little borrowing, a good asset base and steady rental income, all of which allows it now to take on new development with some confidence.

The next major development will be the new retail, community and healthcare centre in the Ballybeen estate, being developed in partnership with Castlereagh Borough Council and the South and East Belfast Health and Social Services Trust. This will cost in excess of £2 million and funding is being made available from the Department for Social Development and the International Fund for Ireland. The health trust is also making a considerable investment of £500,000 in the project.

When complete the centre will consist of a number of retail units, a new day support facility for vulnerable elderly people and community facilities managed by the council. At this early stage most of the space is already agreed for letting with only a couple of small retail units remaining.

The board of Landmark East are also now 'taking stock' and giving serious thought to future strategy. As a key aim of the company is to make a profit which can be used for future regeneration, they are giving consideration to issues such as geographical areas considered for development, attitude to risk and level of borrowing and recognise that future developments may differ greatly from what they have attempted to date.

Lessons learned

Maurice Kinkead, now Chief Executive of Landmark East, acknowledges that the company remains on a steep learning curve as a property developer.

However, with an excellent board of directors with significant property development experience, added to the direct experience gained over the past seven years, he is confident that they can rise to the challenge of building a profitable property development company which will help sustain the urban regeneration task in east Belfast for many years to come.

Among the many lessons learned he would highlight the following:

There's no such thing as 'free money'. Landmark East would still only be an idea had it not been for support from

Maurice Kinkead consults Avalon House plans with architect Ruth Patterson

a range of funders, but it has learned the hard way that such funding still comes with a cost. The application process can be very time consuming, obviously with no guarantee of success, and it can spread over several years, especially where joint funders are involved.

Different funders of the same project can also have different (and potentially conflicting) criteria. There is also a heavy commitment to comply with funders' requirements. The important lessons from this are to read the small print – even 'friendly' funders may enforce it – and to allow for the resources needed to fully comply with the funder's requirements (which are often much more onerous than those of a bank).

Develop strong relationships built on trust between board and managers. It is not 'normal' to run a small business like Landmark East with three paid professional managers and 10 voluntary directors. However, to make best use of the range of skills and experience of directors and yet make decisions effectively and sometimes very quickly, requires clear processes and a high degree of trust and confidence in management staff. Otherwise decision-making either becomes unwieldy or directors are bypassed, neither of which are acceptable.

Don't cut corners on professional advice. Running a property development company requires expert professional advice, from architects, surveyors, solicitors, accountants; don't do this on the cheap. By all means look for value for money, but again Landmark East has learned the hard way that you get very little for nothing; pay for your professional advice and then accept nothing but the very best quality of service.

Don't be afraid of being opportunistic. Don't forget the opposite of opportunism is failing to take opportunities. Alongside all the skill and hard work, you also need a good eye for an opportunity and the ability to move with some agility to take it.

East Belfast Partnership

The East Belfast Partnership, the 'parent company' of Landmark East, has for the past ten years been delivering an inter-sectoral regeneration strategy for the East Belfast area. One of five such partnerships in the city, it brings together local elected representatives with those from the community, private and public sectors.

With core financial support coming from the Department of Social Development through the Belfast Regeneration Office, the Partnership has a key role in delivering the department's Neighbourhood Renewal programme. However, it also delivers a number of other programmes funded by a range of funding agencies including a major health information project funded by the Big Lottery Fund.

Soon after its formation the Partnership put in place a strategy to ensure its own sustainability, recognising both the long term nature of the regeneration task and the relative insecurity of statutory funding. Key to this strategy was the formation of a number of social economy projects.

In addition to Landmark East, the Partnership also owns Avec Solutions, an ICT business. It also established East Belfast Publishing, which published a weekly paid-for newspaper, which closed without reaching profitability after almost two years.

An espresso bar with an integrated tourist information point was also established, although the catering side of this has now been licensed to a former employee and is now operating very successfully in Bloomfield House.

In 2005, the Partnership brought all its social economy activities together in a new company, the East Belfast Social Economy Company, with a dedicated board of directors committed to managing the businesses effectively in order to maximise profit for the Partnership.

East Belfast Partnership
E: info@eastbelfast.com
W: www.eastbelfast.com

Avalon House

Buy-to-let has become all the rage in recent years for the private investor. With a shaky stock market, it has been seen as an alternative way to secure both income and capital growth. But is this an opportunity that community and voluntary organisations can or should take? The Oasis Centre in east Belfast certainly thinks so.

Oasis Housing is a relative newcomer to the buy-to-let housing market, buying its first house in September 2003, but already its portfolio has grown to six houses with a further four ready to be added in coming months.

Oasis Housing

Community buy-to-let housing

According to Oasis Director, Cliff Kennedy, it all started with a gift of £80,000 from a church in the USA that heard of the work Oasis was doing in a disadvantaged area of east Belfast and the plans they had for creating employment and developing income through social economy activity.

Oasis was running a number of successful employment related training programmes and already had a café and associated catering service operating as a going concern on a social economy model.

As it explored a number of ideas for establishing new businesses, it was also looking at how best to utilise the gift of £80,000. While a very generous gift, £80,000 could disappear very quickly funding a project addressing social needs, but the Oasis board wanted this significant gift to have a more lasting effect.

The board of directors were also acutely aware of the poor state of much housing in inner east Belfast and the demand for good quality and good value rental housing. Bringing these two thoughts together, using the capital to purchase houses for renting seemed the perfect answer.

Oasis's first steps into the market were understandably somewhat tentative. It bought a terrace house needing some minor refurbishment for £36,000, spending a further £4,000 to bring it up to the required standard for letting. This was let quite quickly and suddenly the business was up and running.

In a rapidly rising property market, it was then able to remortgage its first property, releasing the total cost of buying and repairing the first house, and then began buying a number of other properties.

To do so Oasis formed a new company, called simply Oasis Housing. It then approached an experienced buy-to-let mortgage provider, and used its start-up capital to contribute the 15% required to obtain 85% mortgages on further properties.

Facts & Figures

Oasis Housing
Company limited by guarantee
102-108 Castlereagh Street
Belfast
BT5 4NJ

T: 028 9087 2277
F: 028 9087 2278
E: thewaterhole@oasis-ni.org
W: www.oasis-ni.org

Contact person: Cliff Kennedy
E: cliff.kennedy@oasis-ni.org

Financial information
Asset value: £525,000
Borrowing: £319,000
Rental income: £27,000
Employees: 1 p/t

Property
6 terrace properties in east Belfast, ranging in value from £75,000 to £120,000

Oasis Housing has now added a further five houses to its original purchase and has found tenants for all virtually as soon as they were available for renting. All the houses are in inner east Belfast although that will not necessarily always be the case in future.

Some of the houses bought have required some updating, such as new windows or a new kitchen, while others have been ready to move into virtually immediately, perhaps with a little redecoration.

So far the remortgaging based on rising property value has worked well as the current six houses and the proposed four additional houses are all being financed using the initial £80,000 investment. The £80,000, together with the capital released by remortgaging as property values have risen, covers the 15% required as a deposit with the other 85% being provided by the mortgage lender.

The only requirement is that the proposed rental income be equal to or greater than 125% of the interest due on the loan. To date this has not been a problem, although as house prices rise more than rental levels it may become an issue for future purchases.

The main reason for the 125% requirement is to ensure that interest payments can be met when void periods and repairs are taken into account, although to date Oasis has been very fortunate in that voids have been kept to a minimum and no major repairs have been required. The mortgages are also on an 'interest only' basis to ensure adequate cashflow and enable the portfolio to grow.

Difficulties

To date Oasis Housing has faced very little difficulty in setting up and managing its business. Whether this is more down to 'beginner's luck' or good planning and management, time will tell. Certainly the directors are aware of some of the potential problems which can, and at some stage probably will, arise.

Finding tenants does not appear to have been a problem although obviously if this did become a problem in the future it would raise some financial difficulties. However, according to Cliff Kennedy, they are working hard to make sure this does not arise: "We are confident that there is long term demand for rental property in this area. We are also being careful about what kind of property we buy and then making sure we provide an excellent quality of service to all our tenants.

"We are also aware that we might get some 'bad tenants' although hopefully we can manage that situation carefully and sensitively if it does arise. We will always try to work with tenants to resolve any issues, although at the end of the day we cannot afford to rent out property for nothing."

Oasis has also considered the implications of a collapse in the property market in Belfast, although all the advice they are getting is that this is unlikely to happen. "Even if it does," adds Cliff, "it would only affect us if we needed to sell which we don't think will be the case. We don't expect a drop in property values would decrease the demand for rental property in this area."

'We are being careful about what kind of property we buy and then making sure we provide an excellent quality of service to all our tenants'

One other difficulty, faced by many social enterprises, is that of work overload, as the Oasis Housing project was simply added to the workload of existing staff. However, with support from Invest NI it has now been able to appoint a part time person working solely on the housing which is viewed as critical if the project is to develop and be effectively managed.

Plans for the future

While the business has grown relatively quickly since starting just over two years ago, Oasis hopes that it will continue to grow steadily in years to private and voluntary sector customers. The centre is pleased that much of this was repeat business, a clear sign that customers are satisfied with the quality of the service they receive.

Income from contract customers rose by 41% year on year, with total revenues on target to reach £1/4 million, which will be a record year for the business.

The generated income now covers in excess of 90% of total running costs of the Business Centre, making it almost self sufficient, an excellent achievement for an organisation whose primary purpose is of support to provide quality training and employment opportunities.

As Alan Thomson explains, this purpose always has to take centre stage: "It is easy to forget that this group of marginalised people have, historically, been excluded from the labour market and have not been given the vocational opportunities that people without disability can access.

"In our organisation, people have a choice to undertake training and to develop their employment skills. Every trainee who comes here is allocated a package of support which includes vocational profiling, access to nationally accredited qualifications and close support in respect of all employment options. It is important to emphasise that choice and support towards economic independence is at the heart of our work. This is a fundamental tenet for us, because Orchardville was founded by parents and carers and to this day our executive committee comprises a combination of parents, carers and professional supporters of the organisation."

Challenges

Business skills: the Orchardville management team believe that developing business skills poses their greatest challenge as, given their previous experience in the voluntary sector, they have had to work hard at developing their business acumen and abilities

Funding: existing funders remain very supportive and have been impressed at how the Business Centre is operating, especially as it now covers around 90% of its running costs. While the Society fully supports accountability for the public purse there are concerns that reporting requirements do not fully take into account business priorities within the wider social economy environment.

Managing a multi-site operation: with the development of a range of social economy initiatives, Orchardville is now operating from different sites across south and east Belfast. This has raised a number of management and communication issues which are being addressed.

'Every trainee who comes here is allocated a package of support which includes vocational profiling, access to nationally accredited qualifications and close support in respect of all employment options'

Future plans

For Alan Thomson, the keyword for the future is sustainability: "Our target for the Business Centre is to make it fully self sustaining in terms of earned income. We never imagined this would be possible when we first started out, but now we are very close to achieving it and it would be a remarkable achievement for us to meet all our running costs through our trading income."

Orchardville may not stop there, for Alan is aware that funding for the Society's core activities is not guaranteed, even though funders are very happy with performance to date. He explains: "With reductions in European funding and changes through the review of public administration our future funding is somewhat insecure. We therefore want to see our social economy activity not just being self-sufficient, but also contributing to the core costs of Orchardville itself."

Lessons learned

It is imperative that in the future, business plans are in place at the beginning of each project, rather than two or three years down the line. In some respects Orchardville Business Centre 'fell into' social economy activity by seeking more imaginative ways to meet the needs of trainees and students. That it has ultimately succeeded is to be commended, but having a clear plan in place from the outset would have made for a smoother path.

The Business Centre has developed a successful business recipe based on delivering a specialised service that is competitively priced and carries a hallmark of quality. Its future success depends on maintaining this level of service and in carrying it through to new markets. It is important that all potential channels to market are explored, assessed and developed, including auditing current marketing practices and business development roles and making new resources and personnel available where necessary.

Orchardville Society

The Orchardville Society was formed in 1981 and is now in its 25th anniversary year. This voluntary organisation is a registered charity that provides vocational and employment services to people with learning disabilities throughout south and east Belfast. Today it is one of the largest employers within the inner east Belfast community, with around 50 employees and over 200 trainees involved in a variety of projects throughout its designated area.

The Society has grown from small beginnings. It started as a voluntary organisation set up by the parents and carers of young people with learning difficulties. Their desire was to add value to what was being provided by the statutory agencies by giving young people the training and life skills necessary to participate fully within the work environment.

Over the years, it has grown to become a large and dynamic organisation and has helped numerous young people to fulfil their dreams and ambitions. However, Orchardville remains true to its founding principles and still relies on the voluntary commitment of its board members, led by the current chairman, George Moore, MBE.

Orchardville has undergone major change in recent years, particularly with its move into social economy activity. The primary reason for doing this was to provide even better training and employment opportunities for trainees and students, but it has also enabled the Society to develop new income streams to supplement its BSP grant income.

At present, income is generated by three social enterprises within the core organisation. Orchardville Business Centre is the business support operation with around 40 trainees, based on the Ravenhill Road. Orchardville Company operates a bottle sorting plant at Knockbracken Healthcare Park in south Belfast. It provides a service to many of the bottled drinks suppliers in Northern Ireland and currently employs three young people and provides vocational training for 18 trainees.

Edgcumbe Catering operates a corporate commercial catering service and is an extension of the Society's two cafés, the Edgcumbe on the Woodstock Road and the Orchard on the Malone Road. It has grown significantly in recent years and now has five people employed in its catering operation and 22 trainees.

For Director Alan Thomson, the social economy programme is an integral part of the society's core social programmes: "I think the most important thing about our social economy activity is that it creates the opportunity for young people with a learning disability in east Belfast to gain valuable work experience within a very stable working environment.

"Our training portfolio reflects the range of services that people with disabilities can provide, so for example, the Business Centre helps to develop back office and administration skills, while our catering division focuses on a completely different range of aptitudes. The bottle sorting, which is our most longstanding community business, provides employment opportunities mostly for young men from east Belfast. Together, these businesses provide an invaluable range of opportunities for our trainees and ex-trainees and they are a vital part of our overall service offering."

During the past year total turnover for the Orchardville Society reached £1 million for the first time. This is a superb achievement and is a wonderful reflection of the energy and commitment of all involved. The Society is confident that it will continue to grow and develop new services to help those with learning difficulties across south and east Belfast.

Judging by its success, having a pint in the John Hewitt is a very pleasant experience. However, for many, the pleasure is deepened by knowing that some of the profit on that thirst-quenching point has gone to a good cause.

The John Hewitt has forged strong links with Casa de la Cultura, an arts centre based in the Cotorro district of Havana. Last year, as a measure of this growing relationship, the arts centre received generous financial assistance to purchase equipment and refurbish its community theatre – thanks to profits generated by the pub.

The John Hewitt

More than just a great pub

One might well question the business or economic benefits of linking up projects between two very culturally diverse cities like Belfast and Havana, but the answer is quite simple. Unlike most social economy projects throughout the island, The John Hewitt is not just a local venture meeting local needs but a place very much associated with the arts and with progressive social and political debate – quite a feat in a segregated city such as Belfast which is not particularly renowned for inclusive and open debate!

And it has a growing reputation of hosting international musicians and acts and supporting international causes, prompted by its founder, Brendan Mackin, a lifelong trade unionist who has built up key international links over many years.

According to Brendan, who is also widely recognised as a founding father of the burgeoning social economy movement in the province, the original idea for the city centre pub was first hatched in the mid-1990s – and the story goes like this. One afternoon, while returning from lunch with some colleagues, Brendan stopped to view a rundown building that had been derelict for many years. Formerly occupied by the Belfast News Letter, it was located in Donegall Street, an area in the centre of the city that had suffered numerous bombings during 25 years of community and political strife.

In a moment of inspiration, Brendan turned to his colleagues and prophetically said, "That would make a great pub." And so was planted the seed for what has become a much acclaimed pub and restaurant frequented by patrons from across the city and beyond.

Difficulties and challenges

While the vision of what was possible came, as visions usually do, without much forethought or planning, the task of developing the project with staff and board members of the parent organisation – the Belfast Unemployed Resource Centre (BURC) – was long and often arduous.

This voluntary organisation had been set up by the trade union movement to promote the interests and benefits of unemployed people and other socially and economically disadvantaged groups. Strategically, BURC had acquired previously rented premises in 1984 in Donegall Street, which at

Facts & Figures

The John Hewitt Bar and Restaurant
51 Donegall Street
Belfast
BT1 2FH
T: 028 9023 3768
E: info@thejohnhewitt.com
W: www.thejohnhewitt.com

Contact person: Brendan Mackin
E: brendan.mackin@burc.org

Financial information
Market value of business: £1.5 million
Turnover (2005): £850,000
Profit: (2005) £85,000 to charitable causes
Employees: 2 f/t, 14 p/t

the time was displaying the characteristics of an area in physical decline and despair. Importantly, in doing so they had developed a valuable asset base consisting of three buildings with no debt attached, mainly as a result of effective fundraising and financial support from a number of UK-based charities.

In the early 1990s, when the empty News Letter building adjacent to the existing BURC premises became available for purchase, the BURC board members approached their own bank seeking finance to buy the large site for development. However, the bank politely refused!

After much deliberation, debate and research, the organisation eventually purchased one of these properties in 1994. The acquisition was achieved at the cost of £90,000 from capital reserves that had been built up during the previous decade.

BURC soon discovered that its vision to establish a new city centre pub in Belfast would be fraught with all kinds of legal and technical difficulties. This was particularly the case when it set out to obtain a license to sell alcohol. To its dismay, BURC discovered that, not only were licensing laws in Northern Ireland very complex, but acquiring a licence was a long, drawn out, expensive affair. Research had shown that virtually no new licences had been granted since the second world war!

But with a little luck, they were able to buy a pub licence for £40,000, even though it was purchased many miles away in Omagh and then had to be transferred to Belfast. And so began the murky legal process of transferring the licence to their newly acquired premises in Donegall Street. The messy process included making payments to other licence holders in the immediate vicinity who often have the power of veto in these circumstances.

In another setback, BURC had to take another publican to court who was opposed to its plans, and despite having won the court case, it still had to fork out a compensatory payment to the objector to avoid a long, drawn-out legal appeal process.

While in the end the organisation had achieved its goal of obtaining a licence, this had been at a considerable financial cost of around £100,000, depleting hard-earned capital assets. On the other hand, it was a good business transaction, given that the average rate for a licence in Belfast city centre is approximately four times the amount that BURC paid.

Enthused with the progress made, the organisation, under the direction of Brendan Mackin, set about consolidating its plans. It developed an exciting business proposal for the refurbishment of the derelict building, including transforming the ground floor into an attractive themed pub at a cost of around £380,000.

Initially, the bank refused to lend the amount requested, but it eventually agreed to an amount of £100,000, which was added to a grant of £25,000 from the Laganside Corporation. Negotiations then began with a number of the top breweries in Ireland. A deal was struck with Guinness, which agreed a preferential loan of £250,000, enabling The John Hewitt to open for business in December 1999 – the first social economy pub in Belfast!

The decision to name the pub after the famous Belfast poet John Hewitt was taken because of his cross-community appeal and local association with the arts. Also, the Belfast Unemployed Resource Centre had been opened by Hewitt, who died in 1987.

the pub has become a popular venue, renowned for its lunchtime meals where customers can relax and enjoy 'the craic'

Since its opening, the pub has been an overwhelming success story with a growing reputation as a great pub. It has also disproved the cynics and the genuine reservations of those, including people within the trade union movement, whose main concern – that the pub would encourage problems associated with the abuse of alcohol and gambling through the use of fruit machines – has proved groundless.

their core business is running a local pub – providing a quality service that will make profits, employ people and support other initiatives to benefit communities

In reality, the pub has become a popular venue, renowned for its lunchtime meals where customers can relax and enjoy 'the craic' – hearty Belfast discussion and banter. And by the way, those dreaded, one armed bandits are nowhere to be seen!

The evening entertainment spot, with live music six nights a week, has been growing steadily over the years. The public association with high profile festival events such as the city's Cathedral Arts Festival, Open House Traditional Music and the Irish Congress of Trade Union Annual May Day Festival have helped to promote the pub as a major player in the Belfast arts sector.

Ironically, it was the area of festival events that led to the company terminating their contractual links with Guinness, as the brewers had objected to the John Hewitt selling non-Guinness brand beer during a city beer festival. But the decision to 'go it alone' proved a positive milestone as the company discovered that it could buy other beers and wine at a cheaper rate, offsetting any advantage gained by the preferential loan agreement.

The John Hewitt operates today as a free pub after the loan from Guinness was paid off through an additional bank loan, secured once the bank had become more confident that the new pub venture was shaping up as a success.

One other major achievement of the John Hewitt is that in many respects it has become a safe haven, not just for ordinary customers of all persuasions, but as a meeting place for former protagonists in the Northern Ireland conflict to engage socially in a safe, non-intimidating environment.

In financial terms, the pub has definitely been a successful business venture, generating a profit in 2005 of around £80,000, some of which has been used to support up and coming musicians or cultural events. Other beneficiaries have included such widely diverse groups as Belfast Kickboxing Club, Belfast Gay Pride Festival and a students' exhibition at Belfast Art College.

Future plans

The company is not content to stand still and has short and long term plans and ambitions to build on its success. It aims to continue develop-

ing its reputation as a popular venue for cultural and festival activity, adding the Belfast 2006 Titanic Festival itinerary.

From an environmental perspective it has also begun a process of recycling glass, cardboard and paper as a 'contribution to the planet', recognising the rapid increase of international beers coming on to the market and fewer bottles being returned.

It is also investigating breaking into a new market with the potential of live theatre at The John Hewitt.

The voluntary directors of the pub believe that a social conscience should be at the heart of all their decision-making. An example of this is their decision to support the one-year boycott of all Coca Cola products in support of the Sinitral Trade Union movement in South America in protest at the company's treatment of union workers.

Yet Brendan Mackin, while recognising the importance of supporting such boycotts on the international stage, also acknowledges that their core business is running a local pub – providing a quality service that will make profits, employ people and support other initiatives to benefit communities.

He has a desire to see the premises expand and – good news for social entrepreneurs across Belfast and beyond – he is investigating franchising the John Hewitt model out to other locations.

It is this ambition and drive that helped to establish the pub's growing reputation to the point where, in 2005, it became the Festival Club of the prestigious Belfast Film Festival. This is a major endorsement for the John Hewitt pub and restaurant, a social economy business that defied all the odds to become an asset currently estimated to be worth around £1.5 million – not bad for a company which will be celebrating its sixth birthday this year!

Belfast Unemployed Resource Centre

The Belfast Unemployed Resource Centre (BURC), which owns the John Hewitt, was established in September 1984, and on May Day 1985 the current BURC offices in Donegall Street were officially opened by the late Belfast poet John Hewitt.

The centre was established to promote the interests and the benefits of unemployed people and other social and economically disadvantaged groups, without prejudice to age, gender, sexual preference, political or religious opinions.

Since its formation BURC has been involved in tackling a wide range of issues affecting unemployed people and the socially and economically marginalised. It has conducted research into the causes of unemployment alongside strategies for employment and recomposition of the workforce. Through the provision of education, training, advice, representation and counselling, BURC has provided an invaluable service to the unemployed and the wider community of Northern Ireland.

The organisation has always taken on a campaigning role, often fighting to expose the broader issue of poverty and its debilitating effect on society as well as providing valuable information on the issues, problems and social benefits affecting the unemployed. Over the years, BURC has been to the forefront of addressing sectarianism across Belfast and beyond and as a testimony to their peace-building and reconciliation work, the organisation has enjoyed the support of both Protestant and Catholic working class communities.

BURC is affiliated to the Irish Congress of Trade Unions and is a member of the National Organisation of Unemployed.

E: info@burc.org
W: www.burc.org

Brendan Mackin

On 14 February 2006, a day more usually associated with red roses and true love, a new and innovative social enterprise was born, the result of much passion and dedication by a local regeneration group in the Donegall Road area of south Belfast.

The TREE project, which stands for Timber Recycling Eco Enterprise and which recycles waste timber into useful items and building materials, was officially opened on that day by David Hanson MP, Minister for Social Development, celebrating a landmark in this community enterprise initiative's development.

TREE Project

Timber Recycling Eco Enterprise

The minister in his speech highlighted the importance of the local initiative and praised the project's promoters: "The recycling of waste materials is important to us all. This waste wood recycling project, which is housed on a site made available by Belfast Regeneration Office (BRO), provides sustainable employment opportunities and skills training for the local community."

He also made reference to the social economy ethos of TREE, whereby any profits made will be reinvested into the community business, and cited the project as an example of what can be achieved through effective partnerships between government departments, other agencies and the community and voluntary sector.

The official launch was the culmination of many months of sheer hard work and dedication by the Greater Village Regeneration Trust (GVRT), a local group established in 1999 in response to public concerns about housing issues in the area, an inner city area of south Belfast that has suffered from serious multiple deprivation and physical decay. Working in partnership with Sandy Row Community Forum and the Roden Street Community Development Group, GVRT aims to ensure that the needs of the community are met through locally owned and controlled projects like the TREE project.

TREE itself is an initiative that seeks to encourage regeneration and stimulate economic activity in the Donegall Road area, while increasing environmental awareness among residents in local neighbourhoods. The mission of TREE is "to produce items of natural beauty, of natural good quality and to ingrain in the mind that to recycle is to regenerate something with value".

TREE is the brainchild of Bob Stoker, the economic development officer of GVRT. Bob, a former Lord Mayor of Belfast and a lifelong resident of south Belfast, came up with the idea of "giving local residents a voice by looking at ways of encouraging their involvement in and addressing many of the issues affecting their lives". Working with Paula Bradshaw he identified that one way to tackle some of these issues was the establishment of a social economy business that "would help to bring training opportunities, economic activity, and investment of profits and overall help to establish greater regeneration into a deprived area of South Belfast".

Tommy Morrow, chairman of Greater Village Regeneration Trust and a key supporter of the project, encouraged

Facts & Figures

Timber Recycling Eco Enterprise (TREE)
301-303 Donegall Road
Belfast
BT12 5NB
T: 02890 233 375
E: info@tree-ni.org
W: www.tree-ni.org

Contact person: Christine Coleman
E: christine.coleman@tree-ni.org

Employees: 4 f/t, 15 trainees

the participation of local residents working in co-operation with others. "Making use of a previously vacant site, the TREE project has created employment, volunteering, training, and work experience opportunities, as well as useful wood items for sale that would otherwise have gone to landfill.

"It represents an excellent example of how communities should be working together for the future good of the whole community. The partnership approach has helped the community share resources and avoids duplication."

From this vision it was generally accepted that a successful social economy business could potentially address a wide range of other issues in the area including environmental regeneration, education and training. After much deliberation it was agreed that one of the most pressing issues that affect this area of south Belfast and indeed Northern Ireland was the growing waste disposal problem.

According to Bob Stoker, who coordinated the project research, their evidence clearly indicated the potential of a successful recycling business providing much needed local employment opportunities as well as generating income and profits: "Our research had confirmed that across Northern Ireland landfill sites are approaching full capacity and the province is running out of new sites to store mounting waste."

Based on this evidence, the trust identified recycling as an ideal social economy business. They determined that an ideal material to be recycled was waste timber, which has varied uses but is often overlooked by other recycling schemes. Surprisingly, for all the public concern about the environment and recycling, the project promoters discovered that their innovative approach to timber recycling was the first of its kind in Northern Ireland.

Funding to get the project off the ground came from Belfast City Council's Neighbourhood Economic Development Programme, which is part-funded by the Department of Enterprise, Trade & Investment through the European Union. The business and operational costs for the first year were secured from the Belfast Local Strategy Partnership distributing European Union Programme for Peace and Reconciliation funds in Northern Ireland.

Supporting the initiative, Eddie Jackson, Belfast Local Strategy Partnership's (BLSP) chief executive, praised the work of the Greater Village Regeneration Trust. Citing the hard work that had gone in to establish the business, he wished them the continued support of the community in the future where European funding is becoming less and less accessible: "As they say, mighty oaks from little acorns grow. While the Belfast Local Strategy Partnership is keen to help establish projects that contribute to the future of our society using a partnership approach and the aim of becoming sustainable, we, as a community, need to encourage individual volunteers and commercial businesses to join this partnership approach so the community business can really branch out – no pun intended!"

The basic nature of the business is that TREE employees collect waste timber from the woodworking and construction industries. This is collected by the TREE TRUCK, a recently purchased new LDV Tipper that has been fully branded with the company's logo and contact details.

The waste timber is then taken back to the business's premises on the Donegall Road, where it is sorted according to its quality and appropriate use. The impressive premises, built

the mission of TREE is 'to produce items of natural beauty, of natural good quality and to ingrain in the mind that to recycle is to regenerate something with value'

on a former derelict site provided by BRO, include a joinery workshop where products can be manufactured, including kitchen utensils, wooden toys, and other wood turned or wood carved products.

Many of the wooden items for sale are made from North American and tropical hardwood and Scandinavian softwoods. These include an impressive array of handcarved wooden plaques, including Native American Indian figurines and classic fruit and acorn pieces that are lacquered and waxed.

Some of the materials which are not suitable for manufacturing are sold through an onsite wood store, as well as being used in particleboard manufacture. In addition, the company can supply household products such as garden fencing or wood cut to size to meet customer's needs. Specially commissioned orders are also welcomed from architects, builders and members of the public.

To the encouragement of TREE, orders have been flowing steadily to their Donegall Road headquarters from as far a field as Larne. Well known companies such as James Brown Funeral Services have availed of the quality products including the purchase of urns, sealed vases in which the ashes of the deceased are kept.

An important aspect of the business is the desire of the board members to provide jobs and training opportunities for volunteers in the Greater Village area, widely recognised as one of the most disadvantaged parts of Belfast. Fulfilling this desire, this exciting social enterprise not only employs four full time staff, but also provides training and work experience for 15 local unemployed people.

this exciting social enterprise not only employs four full time staff, but also provides training and work experience for 15 local unemployed people

These trainees are studying for the City and Guilds Basic Construction and Wood Working Award at Castlereagh College, with TREE providing work experience to boost their future employability at their workshop which is an ideal environment to gain much needed experience. These courses are designed for those aged 16 to 30 years, who are unemployed and wish to work within the construction and woodworking industry wishing to obtain a recognised qualification in their chosen field.

Difficulties

As other social economy companies have discovered to their dismay when attempting to get the business up and running, there were a number of hurdles to overcome before the doors were finally open for business.

Paula Bradshaw, who has played a pivotal role in helping to establish TREE, outlined some of these problems: "We had to convince funders that competition with the private sector wouldn't lead to displacement or loss of jobs in other localities. Alongside this, the normal legal and bureaucratic processes caused delays in securing the site and led to much frustration within the group."

Other bumps along the way included high insurance costs that far exceeded their initial financial projections for the workforce and training elements: £14,000 a year, a huge amount for any company to sustain. Staff recruitment proved to be another unforeseen difficulty, as short term funding meant the company could only offer jobs with an 18-month contract.

Yet for all the problems experienced in the early stages of the development, TREE's directors are quick to point out the invaluable help and support they received from the funders, whose empathy and flexibility helped to boost morale among the group at critical times.

Branching out?

Not resting on its laurels, the company has exciting plans for the future that will help to ensure its role as a leading social economy business in the recycling market and consolidate its position in this field, providing a collection service to companies within the construction industry and 'upcycling' the wood into useful items such as quality children's toys, ornaments and wooden utensils.

In order to keep abreast of the competition and ensure its long term sustainability, the voluntary directors of TREE view innovation as essential to their day-to-day activities.

Included in plans for future development are the provision of a wood cutting service, and the production of wooden briquettes for burning – the TREE Logs!

As the supply of timber increases and markets are developed for recycled products, further opportunities for training and work experience will be on offer for local residents.

Greater Village Regeneration Trust

The Greater Village Regeneration Trust (GVRT) is a local community group established in 1999 in response to public concerns about local need in the greater Village area, an inner city area stretching from Roden Street to Windsor Park, from Belfast City Hospital on the Donegall Road to the Broadway roundabout in south Belfast.

Issues such as affordable and appropriate levels of housing provision, community facilities, employment opportunities and the physical condition of the area all required urgent attention. Pressure had been mounting due to the escalating decline in the locality, manifested through increasing levels of social and economic deprivation among the residents.

Membership in GVRT is made up of residents from the local community, business, political and statutory sectors. Responding to local consultation, there was local agreement that a more comprehensive approach to urban regeneration was needed, in that the housing problems could not be looked at in isolation.

It was acknowledged that the trust needed to be serious in its attempts to tackle the serious multiple deprivation and physical decay and to significantly improve the quality of life for local people in this south Belfast area. In order to be a driver and catalyst for creative and imaginative urban regeneration, the organisation has since been engaged in tackling social, environmental, physical and economic issues, including work related training and job creation.

TREE is also on the lookout for a nearby retail outlet giving them the opportunity to market their goods at a location on the Donegall Road – a visible presence on one of the main arterial routes in Belfast.

Councillor Bob Stoker with Terry McCoy

With all these exciting plans and aspirations, Bob Stoker recognises the tremendous regeneration opportunities the recycling business offers: "We very much hope the community will continue to support our efforts by volunteering at TREE and buying our range of recycled wood products that are now available for sale.

"By tackling disadvantage together, we aim to improve the quality of life for people who live in this neighbourhood, helping to introduce local people to the labour market and promote and encourage recycling."

If all goes well, this locally owned and controlled recycling project, the youngest social economy business in Northern Ireland at the time of writing, will continue to grow and bear much fruit.

Today's TREE is just yesterday's seed that held its ground.

Can you trade your way to sustainability?

With the rise of interest in the social economy and the advent of a less certain funding environment, sustainability has become a big issue for many community and voluntary organisations in Northern Ireland.

The stories of social economy activity such as those included earlier in this book have certainly inspired and encouraged many voluntary and community organisations to consider becoming involved in the social economy themselves.

And as they embark on this journey, it raises the question of the extent to which organisations can become sustainable through trading activity.

The answer to this question is not straightforward, as sustainability inevitably means different things to different people. However, in our experience, one thing seems clear: very few community and voluntary organisations will be able to sustain themselves, without grant aid, solely through income derived from trading activity.

Indeed, for most organisations, this would be inappropriate anyway, as they are addressing social needs that require and deserve the support of government, statutory agencies and the wider society.

However, there is no doubt that the funding climate is changing and that there is an expectation from a range of perspectives that organisations should take more responsibility for their own sustainability.

While there are examples in this book of organisations that are involved in trading activity as a way of delivering their core programmes (for example, Orchardville developing a project to provide training and employment opportunities through its business centre) this article addresses voluntary or community organisations that have set up 'ordinary' businesses with the aim of making a profit and then using that profit to fund what they really want to do in terms of social or community benefit.

In some ways the only difference between these businesses and private businesses is in their ownership; rather than being owned by a private individual or a number of private individuals, the business is owned by a charity. However the aim in both cases is the same: to make a profit that the owners can use to meet their needs.

Case Study: East Belfast Partnership

The example of East Belfast Partnership is one with which all three authors of this book have been directly involved; it has also been chosen because the Partnership has set out with the express purpose of establishing trading businesses so that in the long term the profit from these can cover its costs either with reduced grant aid or possibly with no grant aid at all.

East Belfast Partnership is an interagency partnership established with core government funding from the Department of Social Development with the remit of coordinating and delivering urban regeneration.

In light of a very unclear and constantly changing urban regeneration government strategy, and numerous difficulties with core funding, East Belfast Partnership at an early stage in its development included in its strategy a plan to move towards self-sustainability.

Because it was 100% government funded when it started, the Partnership had absolutely no reserves, as all grant aid had to be fully expended. This provided an added incentive to raise additional income, as having no reserves put the organisation in a very precarious situation, dependent on the goodwill of its banking partner to survive during the many times it waited months for grants to be paid 'in advance'!

The first company the Partnership established was ECOM Management, later to become Avec Solutions. This was initially established in order for Partnership staff to take on a limited amount of external consultancy work; but the Partnership then accessed grants from Belfast City Council and the Local Enterprise Development Unit to establish the new company as an IT consultancy.

Shortly after this, another company was formed called Landmark East. In addition to practically addressing physical dereliction by accessing grant aid to buy and refurbish derelict properties, Landmark East was also seeking to build up a property asset base which, while it would not necessarily generate any immediate income, would in the long term be available to the Partnership as income from rent.

In more recent years the Partnership has started two more businesses, a weekly paid for local newspaper and an espresso bar, although with limited success. The newspaper did build up a significant circulation and associated loyalty over the 15 months or so of publication, but could not reach financial viability before its start up finances ran out and the newspaper closed and ceased publication.

The espresso bar was managed relatively successfully by the Partnership through Avec Solutions, but was taking up an inordinate amount of management time for very little return and the decision was taken to license this operation to a private individual who was also a former employee. This is now operating very successfully for the licensee and also for Avec Solutions, which now receives the licence fee, and for Landmark East which is the landlord.

Unlike the newspaper and the espresso bar, however, both Avec Solutions and Landmark East have proved to be both successful and profitable companies. Avec Solutions has already contributed £100,000 of profit to East Belfast Partnership and is expecting to be in a position to contribute a five figure sum annually in future years.

Landmark East now has around 20,000 square feet of new or refurbished property worth an estimated £1.5 million against which it has borrowing of around £400,000. All properties are fully let, mainly to other not-for-profit or social economy organisations, with a rental income of around £100,000 per annum.

Therefore, at this stage, trading activity has certainly contributed in the short term to the sustainability of the Partnership, primarily by creating a significant amount of reserves which allows it to operate in a much more stable manner by covering short term cash flow difficulties caused by inefficient grant distribution or other unexpected financial difficulties.

Without such reserves, the Partnership would continue to be dependent on bank facilities, which would be very difficult to obtain had it no assets, and would be continually building up debt through banking charges and interest – costs which are usually not met by grant aid. Thus, even with significant and annually renewable funding, the Partnership would have had some difficulty surviving were it not for the funds generated towards its reserves by trading.

So what would happen if the Partnership were to lose all or most of its funding?

Obviously the profit from Avec Solutions could not replace the current grant income, which before costs and various projects can range from £200-400,000 a year.

However, even at this stage, a combination of profit from Avec Solutions and taking all profit from Landmark East without using any for future development, would certainly allow East Belfast Partnership to cover its core running costs with a small executive and administrative staff team.

To some extent, therefore, it is already sustainable, at least in terms of being able to exist and manage itself, and on that basis secure funding where necessary to deliver specific projects. However there is no doubt that its activity would be greatly reduced.

Nevertheless, with the current funding climate it is not expected that core funding for regeneration partnerships will cease and there is certainly scope for both Avec Solutions and Landmark East to continue to develop and build to a position where they can become more profitable in the future.

Landmark East in particular has significant potential as it is already working on a project which will double the space under its ownership and management from 20,000 to 40,000 square feet and add perhaps another million pounds to its asset base.

Both companies are currently undergoing strategic review in which they will look at the most effective way of developing so as to benefit their 'owner' East Belfast Partnership.

In one sense, therefore, trading activity has already contributed practically to East Belfast Partnership's sustainability by allowing it to operate with a significant cash reserve and, if necessary, the trading activity would be in a position now to completely fund the Partnership but with a greatly reduced operation and staff team.

However the plan over the next five to ten years certainly has the potential of creating assets and profits which could potentially fully fund the activity of East Belfast Partnership or indeed any other organisation of a similar size and nature should the Partnership for whatever reason cease to exist.

if necessary, the trading activity would be in a position now to completely fund the Partnership but with a reduced operation

Conclusion

The above case study certainly demonstrates that trading your way to sustainability is not only theoretically possible but it is also a practical reality. However, it is definitely not a possibility for every voluntary or community organisation.

The nature of voluntary and community activity is such that it is addressing deep and real needs within society. It is right that this continues to be funded and unrealistic that anyone should expect them to be funded solely or even mainly by establishing businesses.

It also needs to be recognised that East Belfast Partnership was perhaps in a unique situation given the broad range of people with skills and experience who were involved from the beginning, both as board members and as management staff.

Trading to sustainability is possible, but certainly not for everyone.

Grants: Good for business, bad for business?

None of the social economy businesses that we have been involved in developing would have started without grant funding of some kind. In that respect grants have not only been good for the business, but essential.

However, that said, our experience is also that grants can pose a number of challenges and difficulties for social economy businesses, which if not faced effectively, can also cause serious damage.

Our experience with funders over the years has generally been very positive. However, this has not always been the case, especially as funding mechanisms initially established to address social need have struggled to take account of the different requirements for funding businesses, albeit within the social economy.

This article is an attempt to share our experiences in a way which may be practically helpful to others.

Challenges

Among the many challenges faced by those social economy businesses that receive grant aid, challenges which we have experienced ourselves or have been recounted to us in writing this book, the following stand out as the most significant.

The business plan ends up focusing on grant criteria rather than on the business. Funders often have very specific requirements relating to how their funding can be used, which can relate to the type of business supported, timescale within which funding can be used or the particular aspects of the business which can be funded (eg capital items).

This is perfectly understandable, but the danger is that in seeking to access such funding, the business plan can, even subconsciously, be adjusted to take account of what the funder expects.

In many cases this may not matter, but if for example a business plan shortened the time projected to reach profitability to stay within a funder's limits, the entire business could collapse resulting in the loss of significant money, jobs, and so forth.

Of course a business will need to be presented in the best possible light to any potential funder (or indeed investor), but it is critical that the plan really is achievable and that those promoting and managing the business really believe in it, not just the funder.

There is a significant cost in complying with funder's requirements. Do not underestimate this as it can be much more onerous than for example the requirements of a lending institution. Such compliance will not add any value to the business and therefore in the midst of trying to make a business profitable it can be easily ignored.

However, ignoring funding compliance is a very bad idea, as funders have the ultimate measure to ensure you do comply – withholding funding, and if this happens at 'the wrong time', you will put the whole business at risk. With hindsight, we would now recommend putting the significant time cost of compliance into the business plan from the start.

Business decisions may require the permission of your funder. Even businesses with robust business plans will need to react to a changing environment, and indeed sometimes react very quickly. Speed of decision making may already be adversely affected by internal processes required by funders but if the decision entails a 'change of direction' from that indicated in the business plan that accompanied a grant application, the funder may also need to be consulted.

Such consultation may not happen quickly as most funders have their own sometimes slow-moving decision-making processes and by the time the decision is finally made the danger may have materialised or the opportunity passed.

The focus on profit can be softened. Normally in any business there needs to be a very clear focus on profit – managers are continually looking at ways to cut costs, work more effectively, increase profit, and so on.

However, you may become more profitable, more quickly, than you (and therefore your funders) planned. This might make you and your bank manager very happy but in some circumstances your funders may be worried and even try to recoup some of the grant. This may be understandable from their perspective but it will certainly do nothing to sharpen the business focus on profit!

The 'goal posts' may change after the grant has been accepted. Of course this shouldn't happen, but sometimes the organisation the funder is accountable to may 'clarify' matters after grants have been made and apply new conditions.

Such changes may be legally challengeable but for most new businesses a legal battle may be enough to sink the business before it is established. Anyway, most funders appear to have virtually unlimited legal support when required, so any challenge could be very expensive.

If things go wrong, there are no 'equals'. If a relationship with a funder does break down you will probably quickly find out where the power lies in the relationship! Usually the letter of offer, which you probably did not read all that carefully, gives significant powers of interpretation to the funder.

Add to this the funder's recourse to legal advice and the reality that they probably still hold significant unpaid grant, and you will soon see that falling out with a funder is not a good idea for your business.

Managing your relationship with your funder

While it is hoped that funders who are supporting the social economy will continue to refine their processes to take account of the differing needs of social economy businesses, there is also a responsibility for us to manage our relationships with these agencies without which we could not operate.

Build a positive relationship with your funder. This is perhaps the most important lesson we can learn, as within a positive relationship many of the challenges raised above can be faced productively.

Such a relationship is often built on the interpersonal communication between the key personnel involved, but it will also help if you can:

Recognise your funder's needs. Funders are also working to plans and are accountable to others. Understanding their needs in this respect is therefore important so that we do not simply interpret every action in terms of how it affects us.

Give your funder confidence in your competence and integrity. Funders want to be sure that their money is in safe hands so give them confidence that with you it is.

Give your funder positive publicity. If they share in your success, they will be more committed to helping you succeed.

And even with a good relationship...

Always read the small print. Do thoroughly read your letter of offer and associated conditions, and don't sign it if you think it will cause you serious problems in the future, although this can be difficult as the offer terms may not be negotiable. In the event of any difficulty you can be sure that the 'small print' will be enforced.

Keep a record of funders' requirements. It may even be useful to keep a formal register of requirements so that you are managing their compliance; that way surprises should not happen.

Make allowance in plan for compliance costs. As suggested above, build compliance into your business plan, especially in terms of the staff time involved.

Two questions

Before applying for a grant in the first place, ask yourself these two questions:

Would we invest our own money in this business? Assuming you had any and could invest it, if the answer is no, then don't bother applying for the grant. If you do, you deserve the inevitable heartache it will bring!

Do you need a grant at all? Don't assume that a grant is required. Look first and see if your business idea and plan can work without one. If it can, the 'baggage' that goes with a potential grant may do more harm than good to your business.

Don't assume that a grant is required. Look first and see if your business idea and plan can work without one.

Ownership, Governance and Management

Poor handling of issues of ownership, governance and management can kill a social economy business, no matter how good the business idea or business plan may be. Yet, if handled effectively, they can add real value to the business and contribute significantly to its success.

The majority of social economy businesses start small, often with fewer than five employees. In the private sector such businesses may be owned and managed by one person, or perhaps operate as a partnership.

But in the social economy sector it is not unusual for such a business, structured as a company limited by guarantee, to have a board of anything from 10 to 20 people, as well as one or more managers who are usually not board members.

The company then also has members (equivalent to shareholders) who may be the 'parent company', which itself can have up to or even over 20 directors, some of whom may also be directors of the business.

Such a potentially confusing and cumbersome structure can often lead to real difficulties, particularly with decision making, and can subsequently leave all concerned feeling frustrated and the business struggling.

Problems

Not getting the 'right mix' between the company members, directors and managers can in our experience lead to a number of difficulties, including the following:

Poor decision making

Businesses are making operational decisions all the time; they need to be the right decisions and often need to be made quickly yet with considerable thought. If managers need to consult with board directors, or even members, before making such operational decisions, it may be too late. Also, even when there is opportunity for discussion at board level, there may be limited time for adequate discussion or even explanation, and the decision may not be the right one.

Ineffective accountability

Managers are accountable to the board directors, and ultimately the directors are accountable to the members, who 'own' the company. Often, because everyone is trying to manage the company, such accountability is missed and as a result the focus on achieving the business targets is blurred.

Inappropriate interference

It is the directors who are legally responsible for company decisions, so it is inappropriate for members who are not directors to interfere in board decisions, even more so when individual members attempt to directly influence staff management decisions. Similarly, it can be inappropriate for the board to become involved in operational management issues, particularly when individual directors get directly involved. Apart from being inappropriate, such interference may cause confusion both within the company and with external stakeholders such as suppliers or clients.

Inadequate strategic direction

Another negative by-product of directors and members becoming engaged in operational management matters can be the neglect of strategic direction. Business strategy is critical to a company's success; this is the core business of the directors and to some extent the members. The easiest way to lose strategic focus is to become involved in operational management, and if the strategy is wrong there soon won't be any business left to manage!

Discouragement and poor performance

Perhaps the most subtle, yet dangerous, result of confusion about membership, governance and management is that everyone can become discouraged, feeling that they are not 'given their place' or don't appear to have 'a role to play'. When this then results in poor business performance, people can start blaming each other, leading to further deterioration in relationships. At its worst, you will end up losing the skills and experience of directors and/or managers and the potential benefit these can be to the business.

Suggestions

Effective governance and management are not an exact science and often depend on qualitative factors such as the characteristics and commitment of the people involved and the nature of the business being managed. However, based on our own experience to date, we would make the following suggestions:

Be clear about structures and associated roles

This is perhaps the most important lesson of all; confusion about roles almost always leads to poor business performance. Broadly speaking, there are three clear roles within a company structure (limited by guarantee), taken on by the members, the directors, and management.

There will always be some blurred lines between these roles, but within each company there need to be clarity about roles and a commitment for each to focus on their respective role. Within the businesses in which we are involved, we have found the following allocation of roles helpful:

Members: Members 'own' the company, and are responsible for appointing directors to run the business on their behalf. Their primary focus should be on company performance, for which they hold the directors (and managers) to account.

Members should also have an interest in company strategy, although they do not set this. If they are unhappy with business performance or strategy they can make this clear to the directors, and while they cannot directly interfere in changing these themselves they have the ultimate sanction of replacing the directors with others who they think will get the strategy and performance right.

Directors: Directors are legally responsible for company decisions and while they may delegate much of this decision making to management they cannot delegate their legal responsible and therefore need to ensure that they have processes in place to ensure that managers are taking operational decisions in keeping with the wishes of the directors.

With limited time, and once they are confident that effective management processes are in place, directors should focus on strategy, alongside holding management to account for performance.

Management: Managers are there to manage the business to achieve performance targets within the strategic direction and operational processes set by the board, and hopefully agreed by the members. They will contribute to board discussion on strategy and processes, but once they are agreed the management focus is on implementation to meet performance targets (and of course feeding back to the board information that will challenge and help refine the strategy).

if relationships break down, then all the strategy and planning in the world won't lead to success

Ensure that everyone has a clear role to play

As well a clarifying roles within the company it is also important to ensure that everyone has a role to play and that opportunity is given for that to happen.

While the structure of a limited company for a small business may appear cumbersome compared to the sole trader model, a big advantage is that you have professional and business skills that many small businesses could never dream of accessing. Someone without a role will soon either lose interest and drift off, or else become involved inappropriately in matters which do not concern them.

Ensure everyone has opportunity to add value

If something, or someone, is not adding value to the business, what are they doing there? Managers, directors, and even members to some extent, should be asking the question 'What value am I adding to the business?'. If the answer is nothing, or not much, then do something about it.

Keep everyone focused on business goals (including social ones)

Members, directors and managers should all be focused on the business goals. Are they the right goals? Are we achieving them? Can we improve on them? Such a focus at management meetings, board meetings and annual general meetings will be the best antidote to wasting time on inappropriate or irrelevant matters.

Do not assume that directors only have a role at board meetings

While individual directors need to be careful not to interfere directly in operational management, managers should learn to make good use of the wide range of skills and experience that voluntary directors bring to the business.

Often the best way to do so is to meet from time to time with individual directors to discuss matters on which they have a particular contribution to make, which will often lead to more effective implementation of board decisions or better recommendations coming back to the board for agreement.

Work on building positive relationships

Clarity and focus are critical, but it is also important to work on relationships. A business in which there are strong relationships founded on trust and confidence will often get everything else right anyway, while on the other hand, if relationships break down, then all the strategy and planning in the world won't lead to success.

Keep learning

Effective management and governance, like everything else in life, are areas where we can always do better, so we should keep asking ourselves where we can improve, and remain open to learning from our own experience and that of others.

Social economy businesses don't get to operate in protective isolation from the rest of the economy; they have to fend for themselves and compete against private sector companies often much larger in size and with greater access to capital investment and other resources. In a crowded marketplace, it can be difficult for small social economy organisations to attract customers, establish their credentials or demonstrate a competitive edge over their private sector rivals.

Adding value to your business with technology

Nevertheless, new technology is helping social economy businesses to redress this imbalance. Business tools and information and communication systems previously only accessible to large enterprises are now finding their way into smaller organisations that are clever enough to take advantage of open source software and other inexpensive technology solutions.

Domain name

Establishing genuine business credentials these days begins on the internet, and that starts with securing your own unique internet address.

Getting your own domain name, such as those ending with .com, .org, .co.uk or the new .eu (if aspirations for your social enterprise are Europe-wide), can cost as little as £10 a month to secure and have professionally hosted. It is surprising, therefore, to find so many small organisations making do with subdomains of their internet provider's address, and printing up business cards or promotional material with BT, AOL or other third-party internet addresses.

When it comes to getting your domain hosted, ensure that the charges include all the webspace and email hosting you'll need. A lot of discount providers end up charging a lot more in the end because they have capped the amount of traffic to your website or they charge for additional email accounts to be set up.

Website

Once your domain name is secured, you can turn your thoughts to developing your website. If you wanted to compete with the 'big boys', professional web design used to be an expensive proposition.

Enter content management. Unlike a traditional 'static' website, in which every page needs to be individually crafted using a web design application, a website built around a content management system (CMS) organises your website's content – text, images and other files – within a back-end database.

One of the main advantages of a CMS-based website is that it doesn't require a trained web developer for maintenance, as it can be updated by regular users through a simple browser-based interface. This ease of maintenance means that your website will be fresher and richer in content, and ultimately deliver better results.

Putting the power of content management into the reach of small organisations is the recent proliferation of open source CMS tools. Popular systems such as Joomla (in which www.makinggoodmoney.org is built), which are free for anyone to download, offer 'right out of the box' all the standard CMS features, including the separation of design and content, secure user registration and content workflow. What's more, they provide access to a vast array of other features, such as discussion forums, emailing lists, web logs ('blogs'), document management, image galleries, and e-commerce tools, all of which can be used to enhance your website and entice your users (read 'customers') to return.

E-commerce

If your social economy business offers goods for sale, then adding online shopping facilities to your website should be part of your development plans. Selling over the internet may never completely replace your traditional shop front, but failing to present an online catalogue and shopping on your website is unlikely to be a mistake made by your competitors.

Like content management, however, e-commerce solutions no longer need to be expensive, owing to the availability of robust open source software applications. A good example is osCommerce, which features a rich set of out-of-the-box online shopping cart functionality that allows store owners to set up, run, and maintain online stores with minimum effort.

Voice over IP telephony

Another new technology that is levelling the playing field between large and small businesses is voice over IP (VoIP) or internet telephony. VoIP, in technical terms, is the routing of voice conversations over the internet or any other IP-based network, instead of traditional dedicated, circuit-switched voice transmission lines.

VoIP is already a proven technology and has become the immediate future of telephony: a couple of years ago, only 4% of UK business phone lines used it, but by 2008 it is estimated that nearly half of all business calls will be VoIP-based. More and more internet service providers are offering VoIP as part of their broadband packages.

Driving this rapid take-up of VoIP telephony is the promise of cheap phone calls: VoIP to VoIP calls are free, and links to traditional phone networks are currently around 1p per minute, including to many overseas destinations.

Everyone will benefit from less expensive phone billls, but the greatest advantage of VoIP to the small social economy business is the added value it brings in terms of features that used to only be available with very expensive phone systems and call centre software. Because a VoIP-based phone system is completely integrated with existing computer networks, it runs as an easy-to-use and configurable software application, allowing advanced and customised communications programmes to be set up.

With a VoIP phone system, even the smallest of companies could offer such features as unlimited voicemail boxes, auto-attendants with different menu levels and functions, advanced call routing, and so on. The phone system can also be integrated with other applications such as a customer database or groupware like Microsoft Outlook, offering users screen alerts and innformation for incoming calls or one-click dialling. These are the kinds of features that have always separated 'blue chip' operations from small businesses, and they may prove helpful to your own social enterprise in fighting for market share.

In addition, with VoIP multiple sites and remote workers can be brought into the main office phone system, with free inter-office calls. Support costs are also kept to a minimum because the system can be maintained in the same way as the rest of the computer network, and the software and configuration can easily be backed up like any other network data in case of system failure.

it can be a relatively inexpensive matter to project a strong image for your social economy business

Implementing a new VoIP phone system from scratch can't exactly be considered cheap, as the hardware, in terms of individual telephone handsets, is roughly comparable in price to traditional phone systems. The overall price is kept down, however, thanks again to the availability of open source application software such as Asterisk, which offer all the features of an expensive, proprietary phone solution. Lower support and phone costs will also pay off in the long run.

Any social economy business considering investing in a phone system would do well to consider the added features and business value that a VoIP system could offer.

CRM

Customer relationship management, or CRM, is an industry term for software solutions that help enterprise businesses manage customer relationships in an organised way. A common example of a CRM system is a database containing detailed customer information that managers, salespeople and support staff can refer to in order to match customer needs with products, inform customers of service requirements, and so on.

CRM systems attempt to capture and track the entire process of a pre-sales, sales and service relationship with a customer. Many software applications are now available that permit you to record this relationship from the time customers first make contact. Good CRM software is much more efficient than fragmented records and filing systems as it can save time in tracking communications and transactions with a particular client.

CRM has long been a buzzword in the corporate world, but the software applications available have usually been prohibitively expensive for smaller organisations to take advantage of. Once again it's open source software to the rescue, as products such as SugarCRM or vTiger provide all the same enterprise features at little or no licence cost.

There is still a large cost in terms of the time needed to implement a comprehensive CRM system and to re-engineer your company's operations around it, but many organisations find that it's a worthwhile investment to make.

Perhaps even more than private sector businesses, social economy businesses are all about good customer relationships – knowing who your customers are, what they want from your company and how you can keep them coming back. CRM can help you retain those advantages of being a customer-focused business and still allow your company to grow.

By putting a CRM system or any of these other new technologies such as CMS websites or VoIP telephony to effective use, it can be a relatively inexpensive matter to project a strong image for your social economy business, assuring your prospective customers that it is you, not your rivals, they should be dealing with.

The following list of books has been compiled by the authors because they found them useful or interesting, or because they were recommended by friends and colleagues also involved in the social economy. While some of the books deal specifically with the social economy, others deal with subjects relevant to those involved in managing social economy projects and businesses.

All the books on this list are available for consultation in the social economy library at Avalon House. The list is also available on the website (www.makinggoodmoney.org), where we are happy to keep adding books recommended by others.

Further Reading

A practical guide to financial management for charities and voluntary organisations, Kate Sayer, 1998, Directory of Social Change, 1873860846

A practical guide to VAT for charities and voluntary organisations, Kate Sayer, 2001, Directory of Social Change, 1900360624

Assessing Business Excellence, Les Porter (Editor) and Steve Tanner (Editor), 2003, Butterworth Heinemann, 0750655178

Balanced Scorecard, Paul R Niven, 2003, John Wiley & Sons, 0471423289

Branding for Nonprofits, D.K. Holland, 2006, Allworth BMSS, 01581154348

Breakthrough Management for Not-for-Profit Organizations: Beyond Survival in the 21st Century, Arthur Levine, 2003, Greenwood Press, 01567206395

Coaching & Mentoring for Dummies, Marty Brounstein, 2000, Wiley Publishing Co., 0764552236

Developing Trustee Boards, Tesse Akpeki, 2002, NCVO,

Developing Your Organisation, Alan Lawrie, 2000, Directory of Social Change, 1900360667

Emergence Social Enterprise, Borzoga & Defourny, 2004, Routledge, 0415339219

Enterprising Nonprofits, J G Dees, Jed Emerson, Peter Economy, 2001, Wiley Publishing Co., 0471397350

Excellence in View, NCVO, 2000, Quality Standards Task Group, 07619915651

Exploring Corporate Strategy: Text and Cases, Kevan Scholes, 2004, FT Prentice Hall, 0273687344

Get Clients Now, C J Hayden, 1999, Amacom, 0814479928

Good to Great, Jim Collins, 2001, Random House, 0712676090

Guerrilla Marketing for Consultants, J C Levinson, M W McLaughlin, 2005, John Wiley & Sons, 047161873X

How to Change the World – Social Entrepreneurs and the Power of New Ideas, David Bornstein, 2004, Oxford, 0195138058

How to Manage a Voluntary Organization: The Complete Guide for the Not-for-profit Sector, David Hussey and Robert Perrin, 2003, Kogan Page, 0749437804

Improving Quality and Performance in Your Non-profit Organization, Gary M. Grobman, 1999, White Hat, 0965365344

Investing Together, Task Force on Resourcing, 2004, Task Force

Issues in Voluntary and Non-profit Management, Julian Batsleer, Chris Cornforth, Rob Paton, 1991, Open University, 020156547-1

Just about Managing, Sandy Adirondack, 1998, London Voluntary Service Council, 1872582176

Leadership for Dummies, Marshall Loeb and Stephen Kindel, 1999, Wiley Publishing Co., 0764551760

Management Development in non-profit organizations, Vijay Padaki & Manjulika, 2005, Sage Publications Ltd, 0761933778

Management Teams, R Meredith Belbin, 1981, Butterworth Heinemann, 0750626763

Managing and Measuring Social Enterprises, Rob Paton, 2002, Sage Publications Ltd, 0761973656

Managing at the Leading Edge, Mike Hudson, 2003, Directory of Social Change, 1903991439

Managing Innovation, Joe Tidd, John Bessant, Keith Pavitt, 2001, John Wiley & Sons, 0471496154

Managing Teams for Dummies, Marty Brounstein, 2002, Wiley Publishing Co., 0764554085

Managing your Community Building, 2000, Community Matters, 0900787759

Occupying Community Premises, Jonathan Dawson, 1997, Community Matters, 0900787813

Organisational Change, Barbara Senior, 1997, FT Prentice Hall, 0273651596

Placing the Social Economy (Contemporary Political Economy S.), Ash Amin, 2002, Routledge , 0415260892

Primal Leadership: Realizing the Power of Emotional Intelligence, Daniel Goleman, Richard E. Boyatzis, Annie McKee, 2002, Harvard Business School Press , 157851486

Self-Assessment Workbook Measuring Success, Quality Standards Task Group, 2000, Quality Standards Task Group

Setting Standards, Improving Performance, Dept for Social Development, 2005, Dept for Social Development

Social Economy: International Debates and Perspectives, Jean-Marc Fontan and Eric Shragge, 2000, Black Rose Books, 01551641623

Social Enterprise in Anytown, John Pearce, 2003, Calouste Gulbenkian Foundation, 0903319977

Sticky Wisdom, What If!, 2002, Capstone Publishing, 01551641623

Strategic Planning for Non-profit Organizations: A Practical Guide and Workbook, Michael Allison and Jude Kaye, 2005, John Wiley & Sons, 0471445819

Strategic Tools for Social Entrepreneurs, J G Dees, Jed Emerson, Peter Economy, 2002, John Wiley & Sons, 0471150681

Succeeding with Social Enterprise, Warren Tranquada & John Pepin, 2004, Pepin Associates, 9748783-1-6

Team Roles at Work, R Meredith Belbin, 1993, Butterworth Heinemann, 0750626755

The 7 Habits of Highly Effective People: Powerful Lessons in Personal Change, Stephen R Covey, 2004, Free Press, 0743272455

The 8th Habit: From Effectiveness to Greatness, Stephen R. Covey, 2004, Simon and Schuster, 0743206827

The Basics of Performance Measurement, Jerry L Harbour , 1997, Quality Resources, 0527763284

The Board Member's Playbook: Using Policy Governance to Solve Problems, Make Decisions, and Build a Stronger Board, John Carver, 2004, Jossey Bass Wiley, 0787968404

The Complete Guide to Business & Strategic Planning, Alan Lawrie, 2001, Wiley Publishing Co., 190036087X

The Complete Guide to Creating & Managing New Projects, Alan Lawrie, 2002, Directory of Social Change, 1903991153

The Good Governance Action Plan for Voluntary Organisations, Sandy Adirondack, 2000, NCVO, 1-719916038

The Governance of Public and Non-Profit Organizations (Routledge Studies in the Management of Voluntary and Non-profit Organizations) , Chris Cornforth, 2005, Routledge, 0415359929

The Model in Practice, British Quality Foundation, 2000, Deer Park Productions, 189935834X

The Not-for-Profit CEO: How to Attain and Retain the Corner Office, Pidgeon, 2004, John Wiley & Sons, 04716 48752

The Practical Guide to Managing Non-profit Assets, William A. Schneider, et al, 2005, John Wiley & Sons, 0471692336

The Social Enterprise Sourcebook, Jerr Boschee, 2001, Northland Inst , 97138990

The Strategy Focused Organisation, Robert S Kaplan, David P Norton, 2001, Harvard Business School Press, 1578512506

The Tipping Point: How Little Things Can Make a Big Difference, Malcolm Gladwell, 2002, Abacus, 0349113467

Third Sector Management: The Art of Managing Non-profit Organizations, William B. Werther and Evan M. Berman, 2001, Georgetown University Press, 0878408436

Understanding Voluntary Organisations, Charles Handy, 1988, Penguin , 0140143386

What Counts: Social Accounting for Nonprofits and Cooperatives, Jack Quarter, 2003, FT Prentice Hall, 0130463051

Belfast Local Strategy Partnership
5th Floor, Premier Business Centre
20 Adelaide Street
Belfast
BT2 8GB
T: 028 9032 8532
F: 028 9032 7306
E: info@blsp.org
www.blsp.org

Community Foundation NI
Belfast Office
Citylink Business Park
Albert Street
Belfast
BT12 4HQ
T: 0289024 5927
F: 028 9032 9839
E: info@communityfoundationni.org
www.communityfoundationni.org

Useful Organisations

Belfast Regeneration Office
James House
2 - 4 Cromac Avenue
Gasworks Business Park
Ormeau Road
Belfast
BT7 2JA
T: 028 9081 9977
F: 028 9081 9823
E: bro@dsdni.gov.uk

Community Action Network
Downstream Building
1 London Bridge
London
SE1 9BG
T: 0845 456 2537
F: 0845 456 2538
E: canhq@can-online.org.uk
www.can-online.org.uk

Charity Commission
Harmsworth House
13-15 Bouverie Street
London
EC4Y 8DP
T: 0845 300 0218
F: 020 7674 2300
E: enquiries@charitycommission.gsi.gov.uk
www.charity-commission.gov.uk

Companies Registry
Waterfront Plaza
8 Laganbank Road
Belfast
BT1 3BS
T: 0845 604 88 88
F: 028 9090 5353
E: info@companiesregistry-ni.gov.uk
www.companiesregistry-ni.gov.uk

Department of Enterprise, Trade and Investment
Netherleigh
Massey Avenue
Belfast
BT4 2JP
T:028 9052 9900
E: information@detini.gov.uk
www.detini.gov.uk

Department for Social Development in NI
Lighthouse Building
1 Cromac Place
Gasworks Business Park
Ormeau Road
Belfast
BT7 2JB
T: 028 9082 9496
www.dsdni.gov.uk

NI Equality Commission
Equality House
7-9 Shaftesbury Square
Belfast
BT2 7DP
T: 028 90 500600
F: 028 90 248687
E: information@equalityni.org
www.equalityni.org

HSENI
83 Ladas Drive
Belfast
BT6 9FR
T:028 9024 3249
F:028 9023 5383
E: hseni@detini.gov.uk
www.hseni.gov.uk

International Fund for Ireland
PO Box 2000
Belfast
BT4 1WD
T: 028 9076 8832
www.internationalfundforireland.com

Invest NI
Bedford Square
Bedford Street
Belfast
BT2 7ES
T: 028 9023 9090
F: 028 9043 6536
E: info@investni.com
www.investni.com

Labour Relations Agency
2-8 Gordon Street
Belfast
BT1 2LG
T: 028 9032 1442
F: 028 9033 0827
E: info@lra.org.uk
www.lra.org.uk

NICVA
61 Duncairn Gardens
BELFAST
BT15 2GB
T: 028 9087 7777
F: 028 9087 7799
E: info@nicva.org
www.nicva.org

SEUPB
EU House
6 Cromac Place
BELFAST
BT7 2JB
T: 028 9029 6660
F: 028 9026 6661
E: info@seupb.org
www.seupb.org

Social Economy Belfast
Work West
301 Glen Road
Belfast
BT11 8BU
T: 028 9061 0826
F: 028 9062 2001
E: rachel@socialeconomybelfast.org
www.socialeconomybelfast.org

Social Economy Network
Units 15 & 16,
Rath Mor Centre
Blighs Lane
Derry
BT48 0LZ
T: 028 7137 1733
F: 028 7137 0114
E: info@socialeconomyagency.org
www.socialeconomynetwork.org

Ulster Community Investment Trust
13 - 19 Linenhall Street
Belfast
BT2 8AA
T: 028 9031 5003
F: 028 9031 5008
E: info@ucitltd.com
www.ucitltd.com

Useful Websites

www.123-reg.co.uk
Easy way to check if that domain name you want is available

www.amazon.co.uk
Lots of books on the social economy

www.avecsolutions.com
Providing ICT and management support to social enterprises

www.belfastcity.gov.uk
Belfast City Council site

www.blsp.org
Belfast Local Strategy Partnership – distributing Peace II funding in Belfast for social economy activity

www.bscol.com
Balanced Scorecard Collaborative

www.businesslink.gov.uk
Lots of really useful information for businesses including employment, health and safety, licensing and taxation

www.can-online.org.uk
Community Action Network

www.charity-commission.gov.uk
Vital and up-to-date information on charity law

www.communityfoundationni.org
Funding for social economy activity in NI

www.communityni.org
Community portal for Northern Ireland operated by NICVA

www.companieshouse.gov.uk
Up-to-date info for companies, UK wide

www.companiesregistry-ni.gov.uk
Up-to-date info for companies in NI

www.cooperatives-uk.coop
Promoting the cooperative movement cross the UK

www.detini.gov.uk
Department for Enterprise, Trade and Investment in NI

www.dsdni.gov.uk
Department for Social Development in NI

www.equalityni.org
NI Equality Commission

www.hmrc.gov.uk
All you need to know about VAT and tax

www.hseni.gov.uk
Information on health and safety in NI

www.investni.com
Invest NI, government-backed agency supporting business

www.lra.org.uk
Labour Relations Agency – essential info on employment law

www.lspworkinggroup.org
A joint site for all 26 local strategy partnerships, who distribute Peace II funding for social economy projects

www.network.auroravoice.com
Comprehensive site aimed at women-owned businesses

www.nicva.org
Umbrella body for voluntary sector in NI

www.onlineni.net
All you need to know about anything in NI (well almost)

Making Good Money in Belfast... on the web

www.makinggoodmoney.org

View an up-to-date list of useful websites
Suggest additional websites for the list

www.prowess.org.uk
Supporting women to start and grow businesses

www.seo-online.org.uk
The Directory for Social Entrepreneurial Organisations

www.seupb.org
Special EU Programmes body, including PeaceII and INTERREG

www.socialeconomyagency.org
A social economy support agency operating across NI

www.socialeconomybelfast.org
Partnership of agencies delivering a programme of support for new and developing social businesses in Belfast

www.socialeconomynetwork.org
A network of social economy projects and agencies in NI

www.socialenterprise.org.uk
Social Enterprise Coalition – an alliance of UK social enterprises

www.sse.org.uk/groups/school.belfast
School for Social Entrepreneurs in Ireland

www.ucitltd.com
Ulster Community Investment Trust – a provider of long-term loan facilities, free financial advice and support for the social economy sector

www.unltd.org.uk
The Foundation for Social Entrepreneurs

Ashton Centre
5 Churchill St
Belfast
BT15 2BP
T: 028 9074 2255 ext 222
F: 028 9074 2255
E: info@ashtoncentre.com
www.ashtoncentre.com

Computer Connections
191 Donegall Street
Belfast
BT1 2FJ
T: 028 9032 4633
F: 028 9032 4644
E: info@computer-connections.info
www.computer-connections.info

Contact Details
of all featured businesses

Avec Solutions
Avalon House
278 Newtownards Road
Belfast
BT4 1HE
T: 028 9045 9000
F: 028 9046 1819
E: info@avecsolutions.com
www.avecsolutions.com

Beat Initiative
9-11 Ballymacarrett Road
Belfast
BT4 1BT
T: 028 9046 0863
F: 028 9046 0865
E: info@belfastcarnival.org
www.belfastcarnival.org

Belfast Unemployed Resource Centre
45-47 Donegall Street
Belfast
BT1 2FG
T: 028 9096 1111
F: 028 9096 1110
E: info@burc.org
www.burc.org

East Belfast Observer
c/o Avec Solutions
Avalon House
278 Newtownards Road
Belfast
BT4 1HE
T: 028 9045 9000
F: 028 9046 1819
E: info@avecsolutions.com
www.avecsolutions.com

East Belfast Partnership
Avalon House
278 Newtownards Road
Belfast
BT4 1HE
T: 028 9045 1900
F: 028 9046 1819
E: info@eastbelfast.com
www.eastbelfast.com

Farset International
466 Springfield Road
Belfast
BT12 7DW
T: 028 9089 9833
F: 028 9089 9839
E: info@farsetinternational.co.uk
www.farsetinternational.co.uk

Féile an Phobail
Teach na Féile
473 Falls Road
Belfast
T: 028 9031 3440
F: 028 9031 9150
E: info@feilebelfast.com
www.feilebelfast.com

Greater Village Regeneration Trust
337 Donegall Road
Belfast
BT12 6FQ
T: 028 9033 3527
F: 028 9033 3529
E: inquires@grvt.org
www.gvrt.org

Kinder Kids
Ashton Centre
5 Churchill St
Belfast
BT15 2BP
T: 028 9074 2255 ext 222
F: 028 9074 2255
E: info@ashtoncentre.com
www.ashtoncentre.com

Landmark East
Avalon House
278 Newtownards Road
Belfast
BT4 1HE
T: 028 9045 9000
F: 028 9046 1819
E: info@landmarkeast.com
www.landmarkeast.com

Oasis Housing
104-108 Castlereagh Street
Belfast
BT5 4NJ
T: 028 9087 2277
F: 028 9087 2278
E: thewaterhole@oasis-ni.org
www.oasis-ni.org

Orchardville Business Centre
Lagan Village Tower
144-152 Ravenhill Road
Belfast
BT6 8ED
T: 028 9046 1561
F: 028 9046 1428
E: bc@orchardville.com
www.orchardville.com

Orchardville Society
Lagan Village Tower
144-152 Ravenhill Road
Belfast
BT6 8ED
Tel: 028 9073 2326
Fax: 028 9073 2328
E: info@orchardville.com
www.orchardville.com

Shankill Mirror
177 Shankill Road
Belfast
BT13 1FP
T: 028 9031 2882
F: 028 9031 2885
E: brian@shankillmirror.com
www.shankillmirror.com

The John Hewitt
51 Donegall St.
Belfast
BT1 2FH
T: 028 9023 3768
E: info@thejohnhewitt.com
www.thejohnhewitt.com

TREE
337 Donegall Road
Belfast
BT12 6FQ
T: 028 9033 3527
F: 028 9033 3529
E: info@tree-ni.org
www.tree-ni.org